*Praise for* Living the Legacy of African American Education

"*Living the Legacy of African American Education* affirms the adage 'where there is a will there is a way' to facilitate powerful authentic symbiotic collaborations among teachers, school leaders, parents, university students, and university professors. It offers urban educators a way to advance educational excellence in schools through a process anchored in a historical African American model for K–12 higher education partnerships. In an era fraught with misguided education reform initiatives, the authors' timely, necessary, and exacting treatise is essential reading for educational advocates within K–12 and higher education working within their communities to authentically improve urban education."—Vera L Stenhouse, evaluator and research coordinator, Urban Accelerated Certification and Master's Program, Georgia State University

"In *Living the Legacy of African American Education*—calling on ancestors such as DuBois, Bond, Muhammad, and Woodson—Croft, Pogue, and Walker offer a practical application of proven strategies from the past. More particularly, the editors and their contributors—in describing TITUS—open a window to what works."—Kofi Lomotey, professor, Western Carolina University

# Living the Legacy of
# African American Education

# About the Critical Black Pedagogy in Education Series

The Critical Black Pedagogy in Education Series highlights issues related to the education of Black students. The series offers a wide range of scholarly research that is thought-provoking and stimulating. It is designed to enhance the knowledge and skills of pre-service teachers, practicing teachers, administrators, school board members, and higher education employees, as well as those concerned with the plight of Black education. A wide range of topics from K–12 and higher education are covered in the series relative to Black education. The series is theoretically driven by constructs found in cultural studies, critical pedagogy, multicultural education, critical race theory, and critical white studies. It is hoped that the series will generate renewed activism to uproot the social injustices that impact Black students.

# Living the Legacy of African American Education

## A Model for University and School Engagement

Edited by
Sheryl J. Croft
Tiffany D. Pogue
Vanessa Siddle Walker

ROWMAN & LITTLEFIELD
Lanham • Boulder • New York • London

Published by Rowman & Littlefield
An imprint of The Rowman & Littlefield Publishing Group, Inc.
4501 Forbes Boulevard, Suite 200, Lanham, Maryland 20706
www.rowman.com

Unit A, Whitacre Mews, 26-34 Stannary Street, London SE11 4AB

British Library Cataloguing in Publication Information Available

**Library of Congress Cataloging-in-Publication Data**

Names: Croft, Sheryl J., 1949- editor. | Pogue, Tiffany D., editor. | Walker, Vanessa Siddle, editor.
Title: Living the legacy of African American education : a model for university and school engagement / edited by Sheryl J. Croft, Tiffany D. Pogue, Vanessa Siddle Walker.
Description: Lanham : Rowman & Littlefield, A wholly owned subsidiary of The Rowman & Littlefield Publishing Group, Inc., [2018] | Series: Critical black pedagogy in education series | Includes bibliographical references and index.
Identifiers: LCCN 2017051615 (print) | LCCN 2018005181 (ebook) | ISBN 9781475808216 (electronic) | ISBN 9781475808193 (cloth : alk. paper) | ISBN 9781475808209 (pbk. : alk. paper)
Subjects: LCSH: African Americans—Education. | African Americans—Education (Higher) | African Americans—Education—Social aspects. | Community and college—United States.
Classification: LCC LC2717 (ebook) | LCC LC2717 .L58 2018 (print) | DDC 371.829/96073—dc23
LC record available at https://lccn.loc.gov/2017051615

Printed in the United States of America

# Contents

Series Foreword     ix

Preface: To Walk Forgotten Paths     xv
*Vanessa Siddle Walker*

Introduction: Building Blocks     xix
*Vanessa Siddle Walker*

**1**    Collaboration Between Higher Education and Public School Educators     1
*Sheryl J. Croft*

**2**    Safe Spaces and Summer Meetings     9
*Sheryl J. Croft*

**3**    Creating TITUS Buy-In Among Various Stakeholders     19
*Tiffany D. Pogue and Amber Jones*

**4**    Focus on Problem-Solving and Deliverables     27
*Brandi Hinnant-Crawford and Miyoshi Juergensen*

**5**    Professional Development and Community Engagement     35
*Latrise Johnson*

**6**    The Challenges of Implementing a Historical Model in a Contemporary Setting     53
*Sheryl J. Croft and Tiffany D. Pogue*

Final Words     59

Appendix A     61

Appendix B: Evaluation Report for TITUS Conference     67

| | |
|---|---|
| Glossary | 71 |
| Index | 73 |
| About the Editors | 79 |
| About the Contributors | 81 |

# Series Foreword

*Living the Legacy of African American Education: A Model for University and School Engagement* is a very timely book considering the widespread discourse around educating Black students. It uniquely fits the Critical Black Pedagogy in Education Series, capturing the key elements of the series, which entails historical reflection to improve contemporary educational concerns.

The book brings to life successful historical practices in the education of Black students, walking its readers through the steps for building effective university and school collaborations. Moreover, it provides a blueprint for strengthening school–community relations as well as strategies to engage parents for the improvement of educational outcomes for Black students.

The education of Black people has always been a concern for America's ruling elite, causing them to spend millions of dollars crafting an educational agenda for Blacks in America. Despite the intentions of these "architects," this volume demonstrates how educators committed to the uplift of Black students can use their creative genius to *inspire*, *uplift*, and *educate* Black students. The book aligns with Asante's (2005) motif that Blacks in America were not merely spectators acted upon but were actors engaged in the process of transforming the lives of Black students.

Historically, the state of Black education has been at the center of American life. When the first Blacks arrived in the Americas as slaves, a process of *miseducation* was systematized into the very fabric of American life. Newly arrived Blacks were dehumanized and forced through a process described by a conspicuous slave owner named Willie Lynch as a "breaking process": "Hence the horse and the nigger must be broken; that is, break them from one form of mental life to another—keep the body and take the mind" (Hassan-El 2007, 14). This horrendous process of breaking Blacks from one form of mental life to another included an elaborate educational system that was designed to kill the creative Black mind.

Elijah Muhammad called this a process that made Black people blind, deaf, and dumb—meaning the minds of Black people were taken from them. He proclaimed, "Back when our fathers were brought here and put into slavery 400 years ago, 300 [of] which they served as servitude slaves, they taught our people everything against themselves" (Pitre 2015, 12). Woodson similarly decried, "Even schools for Negroes, then, are places where they must be convinced of their inferiority. The thought of inferiority of the Negro is drilled into him in almost every class he enters and almost in every book he studies" (2008, 2).

Today, Black education seems to be at a crossroads. With the passing of the No Child Left Behind Act (2001) and Race to the Top (2009), schools with a Black student majority have been under the scrutiny of politicians, who vigilantly proclaim the need to improve schools while not realizing that these schools were never intended to educate or educe the divine powers within Black people. Watkins (2001) posits that after the Civil War, schools for Black people—particularly those in the South—were designed by wealthy philanthropists. These philanthropists designed "seventy-five years of education for blacks" (pp. 41–42). Seventy-five years from 1865 brings us to 1940; one has to consider the historical impact of seventy-five years of scripted education and its influence on the present state of Black education.

Presently, schools are still controlled by an elite ruling class who has the resources to shape educational policy (Spring 2011). Woodson saw this as a problem in his day and argued, "The education of the Negroes, then, the most important thing in the uplift of Negroes, is almost entirely in the hands of those who have enslaved them and now segregate them" (2008, 22). Here Woodson cogently argues for historical understanding: "To point out merely the defects as they appear today will be of little benefit to the present and future generations. These things must be viewed in their historic setting. The conditions of today have been determined by what has taken place in the past. . . ." (p. 9). Watkins summarizes that the "white architects of black education . . . carefully selected and sponsored knowledge, which contributed to obedience, subservience, and political docility" (2001, 40). Historical knowledge is essential to understanding the plight of Black education.

A major historical turning point in Black education was the famous *Brown v. Board of Education of Topeka, Kansas*, in which the Supreme Court ruled that segregation deprived Blacks of educational equality. Thus, schools were ordered to integrate with all deliberate speed. This historic ruling has continued to impact the education of Black children in myriad and complex ways.

To date, the landmark case of *Brown v. Board of Education* has not lived up to its stated purpose. A significant number of twenty-first-century schools continue to be segregated. Even more disheartening is that schools that are supposedly desegregated may have tracking programs such as "gifted and talented" that attract White students and give schools the appearance of being integrated while remaining segregated.

Spring calls this "second-generation segregation" and asserts that "unlike segregation that existed by state laws in the South before the 1954 *Brown* decision, second generation forms of segregation can occur in schools with balanced racial populations; for instance, all White students may be placed in one academic track and all African American or Hispanic students in another track" (2006, 82).

In this type of setting, White supremacy may become rooted in the sub-conscious minds of both Black and White students. Nieto and Bode highlight the internalized damage that tracking may have on students, stating that students "may begin to believe that their placement in these groups is natural and a true reflection of whether they are 'smart,' 'average,' or 'dumb'" (2012, 111).

According to Oakes and Lipton, "African American and Latino students are assigned to low-track classes more often than White (and Asian) students, leading to two separate schools in one building—one [W]hite and one minor-ity" (2007, 308). Nieto and Bode argue that the teaching strategy in segregat-ed settings "leaves its mark on pedagogy as well. Students in the lowest levels are most likely to be subjected to rote memorization and static teach-ing methods" (2012, 111).

These findings are consistent with Lipman's: "Scholars have argued that desegregation policy has been framed by what is in the interest of [W]hites, has abstracted from excellence in education, and has been constructed as racial integration, thus avoiding the central problem of institutional racism" (1998, 11). Darling-Hammond is not alone, then, in observing that "the school experiences of African American and other minority students in the United States continue to be substantially separate and unequal" (2005, 202).

Clearly, the education of Black students must be addressed with a sense of urgency like never before. Lipman declares that "the overwhelming failure of schools to develop the talents and potentials of students of color is a national crisis" (1998, 2). In just about every negative category in education, Black children are overrepresented. Again, Lipman states that "the character and depth of the crisis are only dimly depicted by low achievement scores and high rates of school failure and dropping out" (p. 2).

Under the guise of raising student achievement, the No Child Left Behind Act has instead contributed to the demise of educational equality for Black students. Darling-Hammond cites the negative impact of the law: "The Har-vard Civil Rights Project, along with other advocacy groups, has warned that the law threatens to increase the growing dropout rate and pushout rates for students of color, ultimately reducing access to education for these students rather than enhancing it" (2004, 4).

Asante summarizes the situation thus: "I cannot honestly say that I have ever found a school in the United States run by whites that adequately prepares black children to enter the world as sane human beings. . . . an exploitative, capitalist system that enshrines plantation owners as saints and national heroes cannot possibly create sane black children" (2005, 65). The education of Black students and its surrounding issues indeed makes for a national crisis that must be put at the forefront of the African American agenda for liberation.

There is a need for a wide range of scholars, educators, and activists to speak to the issues of educating Black students. In the past, significant scholarly research has been conducted on the education of Black students; however, there does not seem to be a coherent theoretical approach to addressing Black education. Thus, there is a need to examine Black leaders, scholars, activists, and their critique of the educational experiences of Black students. The Critical Black Pedagogy in Education Series is one such approach that may offer strategies to address the educational challenges encountered by Black students. It is conceptually grounded in the educational philosophies of Elijah Muhammad, Carter G. Woodson, and others whose leadership and ideas could transform the educational experiences of Black students.

One can only imagine how schools would look if Elijah Muhammad, Carter G. Woodson, Marcus Garvey, or other significant Black leaders were leading educational institutions. Through the study of critical Black educators there is a possibility that an entirely new educational system could emerge. This new system should envision how Black leaders would transform schools within the context of our society's diversity. This would mean looking not only at historical Black leaders but also at contemporary extensions of these leaders.

Johnson et al. describes the necessity for this perspective: "There is a need for researchers, educators, policy makers, etc. to comprehend the emancipatory teaching practices that African American teachers employed that in turn contributed to academic success of Black students as well as offered a vision for a more just society" (2014, 99). Freire also lays a foundation for critical Black pedagogy in education by declaring, "It would be a contradiction in terms if the oppressors not only defended but actually implemented a liberating education" (2000, 54).

*Living the Legacy of African American Education: A Model for University and School Collaboration* demonstrates how caring educators committed to social justice practices can transform the educational experiences of Black students. It positions historical knowledge as a guide for improving the educational experiences of students from diverse backgrounds.

It is a welcome addition to the literature on Black education. Similarly to Joyce King's *Black Education: A Transformative Research and Action Agenda for the New Century* (2005), this book addresses research issues raised in the Commission on Research in Black Education (CORIBE). Like CORIBE, this book focuses on "using culture as an asset in the design of learning environments that are applicable to students' lives and that lead students toward more analytical and critical learning" (King 2005, p. 353). The book is indeed provocative, compelling, and rich with information that will propel those concerned with equity, justice, and equality of education into a renewed activism.

## REFERENCES

Asante, K. (2005). *Race, rhetoric, & identity: The architecton of soul.* Amherst, NY: Humanity Books.

Freire, P. (2000). *Pedagogy of the oppressed.* New York: Continuum.

King, J. E. (Ed.). (2005). *Black education: A transformative research and action agenda for the new century.* Mahwah, NJ: Lawrence Erlbaum Associates.

Johnson, K., Pitre, A., & Johnson, K. (Eds.). (2014). *African American women educators: A critical examination of their pedagogies, educational ideas, and activism from the nineteenth to the mid-twentieth centuries.* Lanham, MD: Rowman & Littlefield Education.

Darling-Hammond, L. (2004). From "separate but equal" to "no child left behind": The collision of new standards and old inequalities. In D. Meier and G. Wood (Eds.), *Many children left behind: How the No Child Left Behind Act is damaging our children and our schools* (pp. 3–32). Boston: Beacon Press.

———. (2005). New standards and old inequalities: School reform and the education of African American students. In J. King (Ed.), *Black education: A transformative research and action agenda for the new century* (pp. 197–224). Mahwah, NJ: Lawrence Earlbaum Associates.

Hassan-El, K. (2007). *The Willie Lynch letter and the making of slaves.* Besenville, IL: Lushena Books.

Lipman, P. (1998). *Race and the restructuring of school.* Albany, NY: SUNY Press.

Nieto, S., & Bode, P. (2012). *Affirming diversity: The sociopolitical context of multicultural education* (6th ed.). Boston, MA: Allyn and Bacon.

Oakes, J., & Lipton, M. (2007). *Teaching to change the world* (3rd ed.). Boston, MA: McGraw Hill.

Pitre, A. (2015). *The education philosophy of Elijah Muhammad: Education for a new world* (3rd ed.). Lanham, MD: University Press of America.

Spring, J. (2006). *American education.* New York: McGraw Hill.

Spring, J. (2011). *The politics of American education.* New York, NY: Routledge.

Watkins, W. (2001). *The white architects of black education: Ideology and power in America 1865–1954.* New York: Teachers College Press.

Woodson, C. G. (2008). *The mis-education of the Negro.* Drewryville, VA: Kha Books.

# Preface

## *To Walk Forgotten Paths*

## Vanessa Siddle Walker

"Would the community come?" This single question preoccupied the team as we exited our cars early on a spring Saturday when the mists of the morning dew had not yet disappeared from the grassy school lawn.

We were representatives of an elite private institution of higher education—doctoral students, undergraduate students, professors in a variety of disciplinary areas. We joined principals leading resource-poor urban schools in the same southern city. Together, we were educators whose paths rarely crossed only a year before, separated as we were by the traditional boundaries between higher education and public education. But we had become colleagues in the last year, comfortable together in both university and school spaces and all united by a single commitment. The sign above the school we collectively entered that uncertain morning captured the ties that bound us. The school "cared about all its children," the sign announced to all who entered. And so did we.

We had been part of an experiment to see if a historical African American pedagogical model of school leadership could be imported into a contemporary arena. We understood the legacy of segregated schooling historians traditionally captured in their images of southern de jure segregation and, like other American committed to justice, we lamented the lack of supplies, books, schools, playgrounds and equipment, science equipment, and other fiscal needs that southern school boards routinely imposed on Black educators during this era.

However, we also knew of the proliferating literature over the last decades that documented the resilience of African American communities within the limitations imposed by segregation. We understood the support offered by parents, the institutional and interpersonal caring that permeated these environments, the professional leadership offered by principals, and the myriad forms of professional development among teachers that created school climates that continuously challenged Black children to succeed (Walker 1996; Walker, RER).

In fact, we had been drawn into partnership because of a shared belief that these values of the historical African American model could still be successfully implemented in school communities today.

The question we pondered was thus not *whether* African American children should be educated in schools with caring school climates, supported by their parents, and led by professional educators. Instead, we wondered if the historical relationships between higher education and public schools could be reignited in ways that held meaning for public school leaders. Was it possible for cutting-edge professional research about best practices to migrate from meetings of higher education and be embraced by public school leaders? Could school communities generate conversations that would boost the possibility of children in urban schools succeeding?

As documented in *Hello Professor*, we knew these connections happened in previous years in African American educational communities, that higher education and public school educators frequently shared intellectual spaces. But could these spaces be shared again, separated from one another as they typically are via contemporary educational organizations? Perhaps that separation did not have to occur—at least so reasoned professors and doctoral students at Emory University who were both engaged by the possibilities for connection and ashamed by the current absence of ongoing connections.

We wondered in class, in offices, in hallways, and in kitchen talk whether to allow history to develop wings and help inform the present. We wanted to know if the history of African American professional activity was simply an interesting remnant overlooked in the historical descriptions of segregated schools or if the past could provide a map that would illuminate new ways to support the needs of urban children. For more than a year, the talk percolated.

Finally, at the Division of Educational Studies at Emory University, we set out to answer this question. We spent a year locating principals with shared values and commitments to urban children, learning how to build trust with these principals, creating shared agendas that met needs identified by the school, and building university/school shared spaces for educational talk. At the end of the pilot year, in a culminating event, we would get our first glimpse of how successfully we had worked.

Inside the school building, the bevy of activity offered hope for success. University undergraduates were setting up registration tables and beginning to pass out programs and materials in the brilliant blue and gold folders considered overstock at the university. High school teachers' heels clicked as they walked purposefully over spotless floors to locate assigned rooms, where they would lead content-area discussions in collaboration with university professors. In the cafetorium, breakfast smells floated from the recesses of the kitchen and into the hallway, while giggling members of the high school band began tuning instruments on the stage.

Dropping off a daughter who would soon be performing with the chorus in the opening session, one harried mother asked "What is happening today?" The professor smiled, gave her a broad overview of the plan, and suggested she come back after her appointment. The parent returned, as the professor later noted. And she stayed all day.

When the sessions ended that Saturday at 3:00 p.m., hopes had morphed into treasured memories. School board members, attentively hosted by university undergraduates, sat at head tables talking amicably with each other, university professors, and principals, then rose to shake hands as students received awards for academic performance, potential, or leadership while parents, public school educators, and university professors and doctoral students applauded. Throughout the day, hundreds of attendees—enough to almost fill the cafetorium—marched in and out of classrooms along two school halls as parents, teachers, and professors exchanged ideas. Stakeholders previously unknown to one another engaged new acquaintances as they shared ideas over lunch. They also collaborated on future plans in round tables.

When the organizers had announced the end of the day-long symposium, no one in the cafetorium moved. Taken aback by their immobility, the professor returned to the mike. "We have to go home now," she reiterated. Most had been present since the day began with breakfast at 8:30 a.m. Still the audience remained in their seats talking. "The custodian wants to go home and needs to clean!" she finally added.

Jovial laughter greeted the final remark, and the cafeteria chairs finally began to squeak as attendees pushed back from the round tables and began to gather their belongings. Most meandered out slowly, laughing, still engaged in conversation. In a few weeks, all the participating principals would be summoned by the local school board and commended for their leadership. As participants returned to cars now hot from the afternoon sun, everyone seemed to understand they had been part of *something* special that day.

*Living the Legacy* reconstructs the activities that led to that special day of engagement by university personnel and public school leaders in joint envisioning and planning for urban school children. Specifically, it describes the building and implementation of Teaching in the Urban South (TITUS), a contemporary university/school partnership model that derived its structure from the historical model of professional development in African American communities.

This book recreates for interested stakeholders a description of the model of TITUS. Some of the activities described—such as conducting SAT workshops—will sound familiar, as they represent the kind of activities in which other university/school collaborations engage. However, the creation of mutually generated engagement based on a historical model is new.

As grounding for the contemporary implementation, chapter 1 begins with an overview of the networks of professional African American educators in the segregation era. In this chapter, the cross-national network is briefly described, and examples are provided of the ways it operated through its professional development structure to successfully disseminate ideas throughout its constituent groups. This chapter also overviews some of the central tenets of professional development embraced in this model.

Each of the succeeding book chapters illuminates one of the aspects of the Historical African American Pedagogical Network (HAAPN) model and reviews the ways TITUS reconstructed the ideas in a contemporary setting. Chapter 2 considers the specific strategies utilized to create the collaborative structure that became TITUS. Chapter 3 revisits the centrality of multiple meetings in private and public spaces for cross-talk and mutual learning. Chapter 4 elevates the salience of problem-solving as the outcome of collaboration. Chapter 5 discusses activities used to maintain ongoing professional relationships. Chapter 6 describes the efforts to create public visibility and buy-in. Finally, chapter 7 describes the details involved in creating the community professional development event that culminated the year. For ease in connecting history with the present, each chapter introduction begins with a review of the central tenants of the historical idea.

In *Living the Legacy*, we hope university professors and doctoral students might glean from TITUS expanded ideas about ways to reach, and work with, urban school communities. Too often, universities perpetuate the idea that they are the source of knowledge, rather than collaborators with peers who have equal expertise. We also hope that school leaders and parents might use the ideas to determine which university/school collaborations might best serve the needs of their school populations. Most of all, we hope a new generation of educators might reclaim a professional past that diverges sharply from the current educational landscape driven by the expectations of politicians.

We do not imagine that TITUS works in every circumstance. We do believe it can work in many more circumstances beyond the walls of Emory and the urban schools in the area, if given a chance.

## REFERENCES

Walker, V. S. (1996). *Their highest potential: An African American school community in the segregated south*. Chapel Hill: University of North Carolina Press.
Walker, V. S. (2000). Valued segregated schools for African American children in the South, 1935-1969: A review of common themes and characteristics. *Review of Educational Research*, 70(3), 253–285. Retrieved from https://doi.org/10.3102%2F00346543070003253.

# Introduction

*Building Blocks*

## Vanessa Siddle Walker

In the academic world, the pedagogical activities of Black educators in the segregation era remain mostly unknown. Although they made heroic efforts to teach Black children in their segregated schools, Black educators lacked credentials. And they often feared desegregation, because integration might cost them their jobs. Still, today Black educators demonstrate caring attributes and create school climates that encourage Black children to succeed. They struggle against innumerable odds and work closely with parents to build schools supportive of Black children.

The history of inequality in Black schools is undeniable. However, the idea that segregated schools were oppressive and without talented staff is not. In his history of Black schools, Leland Cozart (1967) relates a history that contradicts the popular image of inferiority during the era of school segregation.[1] For example, the education historian and college president Horace Mann Bond exemplified the resilience of many Black educators within a segregated system. Bond posits that assumptions of poor climates that create inferior people rule out "the salient quality of inspiration."[2] From these Black educators, who themselves muddled through segregated education, came a resilience to train the next generation of Black children. Although difficulties and inequalities may take a toll on education, the educators who operated in the climate of segregation had qualities that lifted their students to great achievements.

It's also true that some Black educators feared for their jobs should desegregation occur. Black teachers and principals—like anyone else—worried about their livelihood, and states in the South had threatened to fire all Black teachers in retaliation if desegregation was forced upon them. The threats they faced were very real, ones leveled at them immediately after *Brown v. Board of Education,* and ones that would be fulfilled with forced desegregation in the South in 1970. However, the ways Black educators functioned within their organizations—not as individuals but as collective agents—to challenge imposed segregation restrictions and to speak collectively about the pedagogical needs during desegregation are often omitted from the history books.

These half-truths persist in some of the contemporary literature on Black segregated schools. Most Black communities maintain a collective memory of the caring educators who insisted on high performance within segregated schools. However, many historians assume that the educators naturally cared for children, as though it were an innate characteristic of Black people. This view ignores the work that these educators did—the professional activities they designed and maintained—to create positive, caring learning environments for their students.

Half-truths yield half knowledge and handicap our ability to use history as a context for contemporary problems, but good scholarship can rectify these limitations. Vanessa Siddle Walker's biography of the educator Ulysses Byas, *Hello Professor*, details the organizational network of Black educators and recounts their struggles as professional educators within an oppressive and segregated system.[3] In this work, Walker outlines the structure undergirding Black education and the ways Black principals worked with communities, mediated with school boards and superintendents, and led professional activities in their schools to create quality education for their students. Byas's story demonstrates that success was not due to some innate caring quality but to the hard work of building professional networks that would facilitate real educational progress.

Figure I.1 provides an overview of the various pedagogical networks that influenced the behaviors of Black educators within their segregated settings. As indicated, African American educators operated within the context of pedagogical, national, and contextual ideas. These ideas, and specifically how they might be applied to Black children, were continuously discussed at the two most important national conventions during the era of segregation: (1) the annual meeting of the American Teachers Association (ATA), previously named the Association of Colored Teachers in Schools; and (2) the meeting of the Association of Colleges and Secondary Schools (ACSS). The ATA meeting provided an opportunity for teachers, school leaders, and college professors to interact; the ACSS meeting served only those school leaders whose institutions had the approval of the southern accrediting agency, the Southern Association of Colleges and Secondary Schools. Topics and people typically overlapped across the two national meetings.

In addition, Black educators created state-based pedagogical networks that addressed more local issues and facilitated state action. Typically, a state

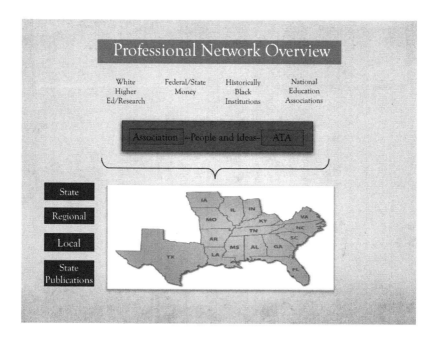

**Figure I.1. Overview of the African American professional network. Courtesy of TITUS Team Archives**

had one annual meeting of Black educators, a series of regional meetings across the state to involve the educators in conversations within their geographic area, and a series of local meetings to address problems within particular schools. The states also published journals describing activities of Black educators.

Figure I.2 provides an example of the array of ongoing professional development activities that state organizations offered. In Georgia, the state organization was called the Georgia Teachers and Education Association (GTEA) and its journal, the *Herald*, was launched in the 1920s. The GTEA meetings a teacher might attend included the annual meeting, whose theme a board of directors generated; regional meetings in each of the eleven regions of the state that provided additional opportunities for the state theme to be discussed; and local meetings—sometimes named "study groups"—where members applied ideas to their local settings. In addition to the meetings of all educators, the school leaders (principals and supervisors) also held state and local meetings, and the organization published a journal to disseminate to members and non-members who could not attend the meetings. By the time it was disbanded in 1970, annual and regional meetings boasted a thousand teachers in attendance, and speakers included people such as Martin

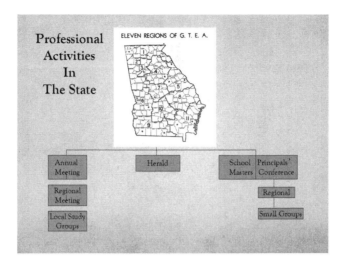

**Figure I.2. Professional activities in the state of Georgia. Courtesy of TITUS Team Archives**

Luther King Jr., Adam Clayton Powell, Allison Davis, Horace Mann Bond, and other noted professional and public figures.

Two points help exemplify the importance of these network to creating a comprehensive, valid historical portrait of Black educators. First, the meeting structure was born of exclusion. Because African American educators were excluded from White organizations at the national, state, regional, and local levels, they created a structure that modeled White organizations in visible activities but varied from White organizations in practices and topics of conversation. Specifically, Black educators crafted into the fabric of their organizations the collective intent to ensure that African American children would be able to compete fully with white children and would become participants in the American dream. Thus, while White organizations discussed educational topics, the Black organizations incorporated both pedagogy and advocacy in their missions.

Second, despite the absence of electronic forms of communication, the networks were surprisingly adept in their ability to disseminate ideas from a national discussion into a local school, or to use the problems of local schools to challenge the ideas discussed at the national level. Across the network, conversations at national meetings could be traced to state meetings, regional meetings, and local meetings. The areas in which ideas appeared repeatedly included testing, democracy and civic education, and guidance.

The networks of Black educational professionals captured the unseen, collective commitments of Black educators that are missing in many historical and contemporary accounts. Yet, when the ATA attributes to Black educators the collective decrease in dropouts, increase in graduation rate, and increase in college attendance rate that Black segregated schools generated in the decades before the *Brown v. Board of Education* decision, it may be that the collective activities across Southern states were successful due to their organizational network.

These networks were expansive in their activities and their influence on Black schools, Black children, Black educators, and Black parents. When the Division of Educational Studies at Emory University sought to reach out to local schools and communities to build the Teaching in the Urban South (TITUS) program, we took inspiration from these networks and the historical model of Black educators. Several ideas undergirded planning and implementation of TITUS.

## COLLABORATION BETWEEN HIGHER EDUCATION AND PUBLIC SCHOOL EDUCATORS

Leland Cozart, the author of the history of the activities of the Association of Colleges and Secondary Schools, provides the most comprehensive overview of the conversational topics among Black educators during the segregation era. By including excerpts of speeches given at conferences, he demonstrates the array of speakers who addressed Black professional networks, all of whom were leading educational figures in their era.

Among the many excerpts from the 1930s until the organization's closing in the mid-1960s are references to the importance of teachers going beyond the school doors to become involved in the activities of the community. "I am simply trying to indicate that unless a teacher gets outside his school room and into the community and takes it into fellowship with him he can do only a small part of his job," posits Owen R. Lovejoy in 1935.

The segregated school needed to "draw a distinction between the world as it is and the world as it might be," drawled Mordecai W. Johnson in 1937. Students could be motivated, proclaimed Allison Davis in 1956, if the teacher established relationships with students so that the "student will identify himself with . . . some teacher." Teachers and principals needed to work together regularly "in frequent and regular staff meetings to formulate for themselves the guiding principles of a philosophy of education," posited W. A. Robinson on Blacks and progressive education.[4]

Throughout these excerpts, Black professionals reflected on issues confronting Black students. They spoke of the need for teacher training, for preparing the children for the future, and of the need to address curricular deficiencies, establish close relationships between home and school, and provide strong professional leadership. These were people like Horace Mann Bond, W. E. B. Du Bois, Allison Davis, and Mordecai Johnson.

Importantly, the talk was not simply among those representing higher education. Table I.1 lists participants at an ACSS meeting in 1957 in Richmond, Virginia. At this meeting, school principals and higher education professionals were almost evenly matched in attendance. Moreover, the commissions, public discussions, and private conversations allowed Black educators across a variety of geographic regions to participate as professional colleagues. This balance is representative of ACSS meetings, where curricular matters were central in the discussions. ATA meetings, because of their size, included more public school educators, although the same representatives of higher education can be located in these meetings discussing similar topics.

Some public school leaders remembered higher education leaders "talking all night" in their lengthy speeches. However, the two groups of educational representatives worked year after year in collaboration with one another. In general, Black educators in higher education and in public schools did not exist separately from one another. The result was that research ideas

**Table I.1. Attendance at a 1957 ACSS Meeting by High School Principals and University Professionals**

| Attendance by State/District | College | High School |
|---|---|---|
| Alabama | 6 | 1 |
| District of Colombia | 3 | 0 |
| Florida | 5 | 21 |
| Georgia | 14 | 6 |
| Illinois | 2 | 0 |
| Kentucky | 1 | 2 |
| Louisiana | 5 | 5 |
| Maryland | 1 | 0 |
| Mississippi | 13 | 2 |
| New York | 1 | 0 |
| North Carolina | 20 | 23 |
| Ohio | 1 | 0 |
| South Carolina | 10 | 7 |
| Tennessee | 10 | 2 |
| Texas | 6 | 5 |
| Virginia | 19 | 22 |
| **TOTAL** | **117** | **96** |

were disseminated into public schools and public schools held researchers accountable for the viability of research plans offered.

## SHARED VISION

Black educators attending professional meetings did not imagine themselves as separate from the students they served. Rather, both the educators serving in public or private Black schools and those in institutions of higher education considered themselves to be examples for the students they served. These educators believed that their students could achieve success because they themselves had already achieved success in a segregated world.

A 1957 speech by the president of Howard University captures this sense of shared commitment and shared promise:

> What is the meaning of the Negro sitting in this room? We have come from the humblest segment of the human race. Men have measured our heels and said what was in our brains because our heels were long. Men have measured the thickness of our lips and limited our minds because our lips were thicker than theirs. Men have measured our heads and because some of them shot up this way and some of them go up that way, and told their children what are limits of the possibilities of those brains. But we have seen a negro with a head that shoots up like a "squozed" watermelon go to Harvard University and come out with a M.D. and Doctor of Philosophy degree. . . . Our existence here tells not only what is possible for us but it tells about the nature of human nature because we have come from the bottom of humanity and we have climbed every stairway that it is capable for human foot to tread. We have touched every shore where human intelligence and the human heart and the trained aesthetic power can touch. We know, don't we? We must be the agents of what we know.[5]

In this address, President Johnson identifies with the needs of Black children through his use of "our" or "we"—used seventeen times in this brief excerpt. He also references the collective desire of Black educators to institute change within their school settings. Each of them, he ends, must be the "agents of what we know."

Black children should be the center of Black educators' efforts in the educational sphere. Owen Lovejoy spoke in 1935: "Those of us who know the minds of youth a little better see that the overwhelming majority of our boys and girls are standing up under a terrible barrage of obstacles and inconveniences and disturbances and meeting with characteristic fortitude and patience."[6] He continues by describing the ways their actions inspired him to respond to their needs.

The shared commitment to the needs of Black children in the network helped create a bond uniting those in higher education and public schools.

Whatever the educational level brought to the meeting, all understood the ways segregation infringed on American life, and this shared understanding stimulated collaboration to address the particular needs of Black children. As captured in a poignant portrait of Black children frequently utilized in the *Herald*, the editors reminded Black teachers: "Remember, this is our *job!*"

## FOCUS ON PROBLEM-SOLVING

For Black educators, the focus of networking was not simply to talk about educational problems, but rather to craft ways to solve the problems they confronted. In *Hello Professor*, Professor Byas explains the need to identify problems within the school in order to actually solve them. He describes and documents the extensive curricular survey undertaken by the staff in his school and the ways he utilized the survey to point out to the superintendent and the community the lack of resources in segregated schools. Professor Byas's approach was successful, and his school received thousands of dollars in needed materials and personnel.

A similar example of collaborative problem-solving efforts appears among principals in the School Master's Club of Georgia, a group comprising all the principals whose schools were approved by the Southern Association of Colleges and Secondary Schools. Vexed by the lack of financial appropriation for custodians, secretaries, and guidance counselors, the members of the School Master's Club generated a survey for their principals that asked them to rank the kind of service their counties provide for their schools. Like the curriculum survey in Professor Byas's school, the School Master's Club survey was extensive and detailed. The actual influence of the survey on the increase in support staff for Black schools in the 1960s is unclear; however, the intent of the survey to be used as a tool for problem-solving is evident.

Professor Byas and his peers felt that Black educators had a responsibility to think craftily about problems in Black schools in order to out-think school boards and superintendents so that the best interests of Black children could be served. Rather than accepting the problems of segregated schools as givens that could not be solved, they brainstormed about school programming, curriculum, facilities, and all other educational matters, and continually asked themselves, "How could we do it better?"[7]

Answering the question "How could we do it better?" involved a commitment to programs that involved Black students in authentic, democratic educational activities and that pushed standards beyond state requirements. In Professor Byas's school, they revised the high school schedule to allow it to model a college schedule, then allowed students and faculty to evaluate the changes in the school newspaper. They tried a Democratic Study Hall; they piped music into classrooms in response to an article Byas had read in an academic journal about learning. In multiple ways, many Black educators were unwilling to accept conditions as they existed and repeatedly sought new ways of improving them. This commitment was demonstrated in meetings throughout the networks.

## PUBLIC RECOGNITION OF BLACK STUDENTS AND EDUCATORS

A regular feature of all meetings, from the national to the regional level, was the inclusion of students. This inclusion ranged from recognition for academic success to student performances of demanding musical works of art.

The recognition of student achievement was accompanied by recognition of teacher achievement. Multiple teacher of the year awards were given at national, regional, and local levels. The selection process included a rigorous group interview by members of the educational and business community. Regional winners were celebrated in a formal annual event, and state winners received multiple gifts and recognition. The winners also spoke at events attended by business and school leaders and reflected on educational beliefs that mattered. These activities, inclusive of plaques and public applause, centered on Black children and those who taught them well as part of the professional network.

These attributes of the Black pedagogical network were ones discussed at Emory in a variety of classes and informal settings, and they provided the foundation for conversations that would create the TITUS program. Although TITUS worked on a much smaller scale than the historical model it emulated, it determined that all engagement activities with local schools would follow elements of the historical model. Each chapter that follows explains how aspects of the historical script were reinvented in the contemporary setting.

## NOTES

1. L. S. Cozart, *A History of the Association of Colleges and Secondary Schools, 1934–65* (Charlotte, NC: Association of Colleges and Secondary Schools, 1967), 30.

2. Cozart, *A History*, 20.

3. V. S. Walker, *Hello Professor: A Black Principal and Professional Leadership in the Segregated South* (Chapel Hill: University of North Carolina Press, 2009).

4. Cozart, *A History*, 95, 99, 117–118.

5. This quote can be found on page 99 of Vanessa Siddle Walker's (2009) *Hello Professor: a black principal and professional leadership in the segregated south*. Chapel Hill: University of North Carolina Press.

6. Cozart, *A History*, 95.

7. Walker, *Hello Professor*, 159.

*Chapter One*

# Collaboration Between Higher Education and Public School Educators

## Sheryl J. Croft

Using the African American pedagogical model described in the introduction, this chapter chronicles how an elite Southern university attempted to create an authentic collaboration and a shared vision between the university and public schools. Creating the TITUS structure required (1) a supportive university climate, (2) a close coalition between a representative of higher education and public school participants, and (3) intentional interactions that would provide a foundation for collaboration.

### SUPPORTIVE UNIVERSITY CLIMATE

University buy-in and support proved to be one of the most important keys to building an authentic university–public school collaboration.

In many ways, the Division of Educational Studies (DES) provided unique opportunities to create a new urban vision. Prior to the introduction of the TITUS initiative, the DES faculty had already engaged in a series of discussions about "how the department should imagine its educational contribution and role in the twenty-first century." Based on these discussions, and as early as 1990, DES had already produced a Twenty-First Century Position Paper in which it outlined its goals and its desire to serve the educational community surrounding the university. Over twenty years after the completion of this paper, faculty continue annually to affirm their commitment to urban schools and exemplify this commitment in their admission practices, courses, support for other school projects, and faculty hiring.

As a result of the division's voiced commitment to urban education, this specific department (the Division of Educational Studies)—housed within an elite private R-1 university—had goals and a focus already aligned with an initiative designed to work specifically with urban populations situated in a large metropolitan area and with neighboring communities consisting primarily of low-income students of color.[1] In fact, Teaching in the Urban South (TITUS) was named by the division head.

Of course, alignment and commitment did not mean immediate approval. When the founder of TITUS (hereafter called "university representative") first approached her faculty members with the TITUS vision, they expressed that the goals of the vision could not be reached with the limited departmental resources available. Faculty felt that the time, manpower, brainpower, and resources necessary for authentic collaborations with local urban schools were beyond the realm of possibility. In fact, except for $1,000, no money could be found by DES, and Emory's other departments provided no funding. Interestingly, as discussed in chapter 3, doctoral students were more optimistic about the possibilities. In a shared planning meeting, the voice of doctoral students prevailed, and TITUS officially launched. After gaining a vision and commitment, the university needed partners.

## UNIVERSITY AND SCHOOL REPRESENTATIVES

Early DES conversations recognized that K–12 personnel frequently perceived university–school relationships as unidirectional, exploitative, and designed to meet the needs of the university. As doctoral students aligned with university representatives (hereafter called the "TITUS team") to create a vision for TITUS, they focused on building bridges with K–12 personnel rather than alienating them.

The TITUS team reviewed the interconnections between higher education and public schools in the segregation era[2] and explored ways it could forge relationships with K–12 personnel that would be strong enough to overcome long-standing skepticism and allow university personnel to enter school spaces not as researchers, but as partners dedicated to working with school personnel to improve education for their students. The TITUS team believed it could overcome the suspicions about universities, and sought to do so in several concrete ways. These included building close relationships between representatives of both the university and schools, and creating distinct assignments for representatives of each group.

## RELIANCE ON SCHOOL REPRESENTATIVES

Authentically linking university representatives and public school leaders required the utilization of people who represented each group, who were trusted by each group, and who worked well together. In TITUS, one of these people had a twenty-year relationship with DES, having been promoted through the university ranks. She was a former high school teacher, and her research uncovered the historical model of African American professional education activities. She became the university representative.

A DES doctoral student had been a teacher, principal, and area supervisor in the school system planned for the TITUS initiative. A product of segregated schools, she brought personal experiences to the scholarship about professionalism among African American educators during the era of segregation. She also brought close and trusted relationships with current school personnel. This person became the school representative.[3]

Importantly, both representatives shared common beliefs:

- commitment to the effective education of urban children
- belief in the ability and skill of contemporary school leaders to educate children
- belief that positive educational experiences were occurring in urban schools
- belief in the necessity for authentic collaborations between school leaders and university personnel
- belief that communities would benefit from such a collaboration
- belief that aspects of the historical model might be replicated in similar settings

Prior to any attempt to reach out to schools, these commonalities signaled trust and credibility between two collaborators whose job it would be to connect their professional worlds.

## INITIAL STEPS IN THE COLLABORATION

As an insider of academia, the university representative used her research and academic status to gain departmental buy-in. As a K–12 insider, the school representative used her prior relationships with principals to present the idea of participating in TITUS.

### Creating Distinct Assignments for the University and School Representatives

Finding a match between the university's mission and potential participants' values and beliefs was imperative to the success of this initiative and bridging the two worlds. This was the job of the school representative. Carefully vetting school leaders who might be interested in involving their school communities, the school representative created a list of principals she believed shared a similar mission, commitment, and purpose in their work with

African American students. In this sense, the school representative's previous insider position as a principal and assistant superintendent, as well as her knowledge of the African American Historical Pedagogical Model, proved invaluable in identifying potential participants. She identified several criteria for selection. They included the following:

- elevating the needs of children above the needs of faculty or adults
- high expectations for faculty and students
- student-centered focus
- desire to educate the whole child
- desire to make genuine connections with the university
- desire to improve educational delivery

These were the common characteristics of the principals nominated as TITUS fellows. The school representative engaged all principals she could identify (based on her previous relationships with school staff in the local district) in preliminary conversations regarding their potential participation. In consultation, the university representative agreed that participants in the program should receive a title of affiliation. Such a title provided formal affiliation with Emory University and could be included in their professional profile. With approval from the DES faculty, this title became "TITUS fellow."

Shortly after the school representative compiled the list of potential TITUS fellows, the names were approved by DES, and the university representative crafted an invitation letter to principals inviting them to become TITUS fellows.

## Preparing the Invitation to Participate

Importantly, collaboration between the school representative and the university representative was essential in crafting a successful letter. The first letter, written by the university representative, provided an academic rationale for the program. This letter was several pages long and focused on the justification for the program using long paragraphs. The school representative, cognizant of the principals' need to access and process pertinent and relevant information quickly, revised the letter. Her letter contained bold headings with bulleted subtopics that allowed for quick and efficient reading and understanding of the content. It also used revised language.

In a telling comment, one of the potential fellows called the school representative to ask, "What is this letter saying, and is this the same program that you were describing to me?" The point is that without the school representative's input and interpretation, the principals might have disregarded the university representative's letter.

## Intentioned Interaction

While the school representative made the TITUS program appealing to the potential fellows, the university representative needed to build trust if the collaboration was to be reciprocal and multidirectional. Because of a deeply entrenched distrust of academia, both the school and university representatives realized it was necessary for the university representative to visit each school personally to discuss the TITUS project. In other words, the university representative needed to establish her own relationship with the potential fellows so they would trust that she aligned with them in similar interest in and commitment to their students.

As such, the university representative had to negotiate how to build her credibility with principals as a fellow educator. Given the prevailing sentiment of many school leaders that a huge gap exists between researchers and their schools' interests, the university representative had to convince these school leaders that she brought educational experiences that allowed her to understand school complexities, that she respected the job they engaged in daily, and that she sought rapport built on shared educational values.

The university representative also realized that if the TITUS collaboration were to be authentic and productive, all imagined or real hierarchal pretenses needed to be acknowledged, addressed, and dispelled. In this sense, a seemingly minor task, such as going to a school to meet the principal, became, as the university representative readily reports, a job that required adhering to unwritten rules related to visitors and parking, using less formal community talk in conversations with parents and support staff, and engaging school secretaries in enthusiastic conversations about the professional activities of their school leader. "One the most daunting of tasks was walking into the principal's office," the representative later reported.[4] Reminded of her earlier days as a high school teacher, she entered offices with a respect for authority that allowed lighthearted initial conversations that generated laughter about principals intimidating some teachers. At the end of one of her visits, a principal expressed his impression of the university in this way:

> Not until meeting the university representative and "researching" her, and becoming mesmerized by her historical data, and getting assurances from both [the school representative] and [the university representative] that this program would benefit my students academically did I agree to become a TITUS fellow.[5]

The university representative's deference and respect for the principals as competent professionals in their own right minimized her outsider position. Her previous research on "good" segregated schools and the ways the potential TITUS fellows seemed to embody the professional and interpersonal skills of earlier Black principals also aided the rapport.

These initial visits to schools allowed the university representative to establish her own independent relationships with school leaders and allowed her to confirm that principals in these schools were, at least on the surface, creating environments conducive to student learning, despite the lack of resources and county support all confronted. At every school, the university representative was impressed by the student-centered focus and climate, the order and discipline, the array of institutional support offered to students, and the attractive campuses. Without exception, each school seemed to be a place where student learning mattered to the principal and staff.

Shortly after initial visits, the school representative and the university representative visited each school again—together. To aid collaboration, the purpose of this second visit was to ask principals to identify ways the university could best serve them and their schools. To start the conversation, the university representative queried each principal: "If you could dream, what would you want to see a university do for your school?"[6] In other words, the university representative expressed a desire to be of help to principals in their school programs, *not* for the principal to offer the school as a research or practice site for the university.

This question and the succeeding conversation:

- allowed the principals to function as professional leaders, fully able to articulate the needs that would help their schools;
- created a context of university and schools bound by a single focus to help children; and
- established a working framework for the university and school leaders to view one another as professional colleagues.

By the end of this second visit, each TITUS fellow had supplied the university representative with a list of school needs that would support the academic development of students in his or her school and had agreed to be part of professional leadership conversations at the university with other fellows. Notwithstanding initial skepticism, each principal, without exception, expressed a desire to participate in the TITUS initiative. In fact, one principal noted that "TITUS wanted to stop blaming and start working toward closing achievement gaps in our schools."[7]

With the schools and university conceptually aligned, the first foundation stone for reinventing the historical model was in place. The university formally named each urban principal a TITUS fellow. The foundation for a close partnership between the university and public schools had been laid.

## IDEAS TO CONSIDER

- Do you have a departmental climate aligned with a professional development mission?
- Do you have a university representative who understands the model and has the school experiences and commitment to link with public school leaders in their cultural location?
- Do you have a university-affiliated doctoral student or other faculty member who has close, trusted relationships with public school leaders?
- Do your university and school representatives have mutual respect, share common beliefs, and work well together?
- Are principals respected as professional leaders and allowed to articulate the needs in their schools?
- Have you designed meetings that provide opportunities for school leaders and university personnel to engage as professional peers?
- Has the university provided formal titles or another form of endorsement that creates status for the school leaders among their educational peers?

## NOTES

1. The school systems surrounding the university consisted of two of the five largest systems in the state. According to the Governor's Office of Student Achievement for the state of Georgia, the specific school system with which TITUS worked had a population of 69 percent African American children in 2013–2014 (https://app.doe.k12.ga.us/ows-bin/owa/fte_pack_ethnicsex.entry_form).

2. Even though *Brown I* was signed in 1954 and *Brown II* in 1955, integration of students was not possible because of White flight from Atlanta; the majority of students housed within the city were African American. As a result, schools functioned in much the same way that they had prior to *Brown v. Board.*

3. The school representative received her Diploma for Advanced Study in Teaching (DAST) (Emory University's equivalent of the more widely known Educational Specialist Degree) in 1998, and in 2008 she, ten years later, reentered the university as a PhD student in educational studies. During the intervening ten years, the university representative (a professor) solidified her research on pre-*Brown* African American schools, and the school/cultural connector completed her tenure in a major school system after having initiated as principal many of the traditions she experienced as a student in a pre-*Brown* school. Hence 2008 saw the convergence of both the university representative's and school representative's paths when the school representative enrolled as a PhD student and the university representative became her advisor.

4. Personal interview with author, 2014.

5. G. Goodwin, presentation at the Annual Meeting of the American Educational Research Association, San Francisco, CA, April 27–May 1, 2013.

6. The university representative asked school principals this question during her second visit to schools, in 2012.

7. Goodwin, presentation at the Annual Meeting of the AERA.

*Chapter Two*

# Safe Spaces and Summer Meetings

## Sheryl J. Croft

To recreate professional relationships and amplify shared educational visions between the university representative, the school representative, and the new TITUS fellows, the TITUS program launched a series of three professional development workshops the summer before the fall pilot program would begin. All fellows attended these workshops. The summer sessions required careful planning. Specifically, the university representative and the school representative worked closely together to create a climate for the professional exchange of ideas and to create and deliver workshop materials and activities that would facilitate professional engagement while fellows delved into understanding the African American Pedagogical Model.

## CREATING A CLIMATE FOR THE PROFESSIONAL EXCHANGE OF IDEAS

The university and school representatives understood that putting fellows in the same room with university members might not foster authentic collaboration. Thus, prior to the first workshop, the representatives engaged in several deliberate strategies to generate shared intellectual discussion and learning. These details included logistics and nonverbal messages.

### Logistics

The university and school representatives consulted with the fellows to agree on a mutually beneficial meeting space for the workshops. Prior to consultation, the university representative believed a meeting space in one of the urban schools would be most helpful. After all, the schools were located reasonably close to one another in the southern part of the urban county, and she believed the decreased travel time would infringe less on their demanding schedules as principals. The university representative was wrong.

When asked their preference for a meeting space, the fellows unilaterally elected to use the university campus. Fellows believed the neutral space of the university would allow them to feel comfortable in conversations that required them to talk about their school communities in confidential ways. Unlike meeting in one of their schools, fellows believed the university offered a "safe space" for frank talk. By "safe," they meant they could speak freely without being concerned about who might be listening or who might report the conversation to a superintendent.

The fellows also posited practical reasons for meeting at the university. Unlike the schools in which they functioned as leaders, where interruptions could be continual, at the university they could actually get away from the stream of questions, decisions, and visitors. "If we stay at our schools," one said, "we can't get anything done."

Upon reflection, the university representative recognized another unspoken benefit of meeting at the university. In a university classroom, a location most American citizens associate with learning, the fellows could also freely engage in conversations about a historical model they each embodied as school leaders but could not have articulated to one another. A university setting gave them the freedom to be consumers of knowledge.

The decision-making on the location of the summer workshop, however, was only one facet of the preparation for creating a climate for the exchange of ideas. The university representative and school representative also collaborated on material details that would communicate hidden messages of respect for the school leaders.

## Creating Messages of Respect

Prior to the first workshop meeting, the university and school representatives consulted with each fellow's secretary to arrange the details of the first workshop meeting. TITUS sought to convey to the fellows its understanding that principals had demanding jobs as school leaders and, following traditional historical norms of respect, did not assume a university representative could simply barge into the calendar of a fellow without working through a secretary.

Communication with the fellows' secretaries involved several matters. First, a university secretary consulted with the fellow about lunch preferences. Although the university representative could have simply ordered meals of her choice for the catered event, the gesture of self-selection was deliberately chosen to give deference to the fellows and signal the university's appreciation for the time commitment fellows were making to travel to the university. TITUS emailed schools' secretaries lunch choices; secretaries consulted with the fellows and communicated back to the university the fellows' choices for meals for each of the three planned workshops.

The university and school representative also communicated with school secretaries about travel to the university. TITUS supplied specific parking instructions to school secretaries, inclusive of methods for payment, to be certain the fellows would have all the information they needed when they left their schools for the first meeting. TITUS also explained to secretaries that members of the TITUS team would meet the fellows as they arrived. These doctoral students would welcome the fellows to Emory and escort them to the building and classroom. The intention was to communicate to the fellows, through their staff, Emory's intention to welcome them as honored guests.

Importantly, communication through secretaries also elevated the fellow within his or her school as a principal who had a special relationship with Emory University. When the secretary was aware of the principal's elevation as "fellow," the status could also be more widely disseminated in other forms of school communication. Thus, communicating via secretaries conveyed implicit messages of respect for their positions as school leaders, while also allowing the message about each principal's selection to begin to be disseminated throughout the schools.

The university and school representatives also busied themselves preparing the room prior to the first workshop. They traveled together to the university bookstore and purchased folders, pens, and writing tablets to facilitate the learning aspect of the workshop. Spurred by the understanding that urban school leaders are often undervalued, the school representative urged adding a small gift to the packet. After reviewing several possibilities, the university and school representatives chose simple Emory mugs for each fellow. At the time of purchase, they believed that the mugs would be used for coffee refills during varied sessions.

The university representative prepared workshop materials for inclusion in the folders. The fellows needed agendas and supporting materials for the first topic of conversation. She created sufficient copies of each handout, careful to utilize several colors to create a more inviting packet, and inserted these into the folder. Simultaneously, the school representative prepared copies of the announcement of the fellows, with their pictures and philosophies, which would be circulated at Emory. When the folders were complete, the university and school representatives carried the materials and the mugs into the classroom for the workshop. There they contemplated the final element that could send a hidden message.

Both believed the glossy folders, each carefully placed with an accompanying mug beside it, communicated the value the fellows held to the university. However, they could not decide how to arrange the tables. They tried several approaches. Rows were not acceptable, nor was any arrangement that created a clear "head" of the table. Although the university representative would function as a teacher of the workshop as she overviewed the historical model, she did not wish to appear the solo authority at a time when the goal was shared conversation. Finally, they agreed on an open rectangular format that allowed ample space for crosstalk between university and school professionals. They hoped that when the fellows arrived, each would feel immediately welcomed into a well-appointed, collaboratively designed, professional learning space.

These seemingly small details of preparation were carefully crafted to communicate nonverbally with each fellow about the university's respect for, and value of, his or her contributions in school settings. The response of each principal upon arrival affirmed the significance of the details. "Nobody ever gives us anything," one principal commented as she picked up the mug next to the workshop materials on the first day. While the university and school representatives had thought these mugs would simply be useful for coffee refills, the principals gathered them as small treasures and never used any of the mugs for coffee. Not once.

## WORKSHOPPING THE HISTORICAL MODEL

The summer workshops were designed for the university representative to work with the fellows to see their work as part of a long legacy of professional talk and action about the education of underserved children, inclusive of professional leadership, parental involvement, and teaching support.

### Session 1: Professional Networking and Strategic Response

This title was printed on each fellows' folder upon arrival for the first visit. After informal greetings, the fellows and university representative convened around the tables and began the work of importing a "lost" model into a contemporary dialogue. Since all fellows shared some aspects of the model, the goal of the university representative was to help them to understand their actions as part of a lost educational heritage.

At the opening, the university representative described the historical African American Pedagogical Model using slides and discussion handouts. She talked about assumptions regarding the professionalism of Black educators, generated during desegregation, and described in detail the deliberate ways Black educational leaders of another era regularly attended meetings with their professional colleagues in public schools and with university faculty to learn about educational practices working in other schools. The ideas the fellows learned were part of the professional conversations of their predecessors and included ways to support teacher development, prepare Black students for testing, think about curricular needs aimed at students, and inspire student development. These ideas were discussed using a chart, part of which appears below.

Despite the time references in the chart indicating that Black principals had discussed these ideas decades before, in their own professional development settings, with members of higher education, the fellows immediately recognized in these statements some of the values they contemporarily embraced in their own schools.

The fellows identified with the commitment to children evidenced in the African American Pedagogical Model. One slide they viewed captured the multiple times the Howard University president, in a professional meeting with Black principals in 1957, used the words "I" and "we" to describe his and his fellow principals' commitment to developing the potential of Black

**Table 2.1.**

| Educational Idea | Statement of Importance |
| --- | --- |
| Testing | Tests have become a most powerful factor. . . . We should not underestimate their power. . . . We have got to learn to stop being mad and be smart. Use all the angles. . . . We have got to learn all the tricks and to work at it. (Allison Davis, 1958) |
| Understanding the Home Environment of the Child | How can we know what a child's needs are or how to help him meet his problems unless we know his gang, his political affiliations or civic interests? . . . I am simply trying to indicate that unless a teacher gets outside his school room and into the community and takes it into fellowship with him, he can do only a small part of his job. (Owen R. Lovejoy, 1935) |
| Leading Professional Development | It is the intelligence and courage of a principal and his staff working together in frequent and regular staff meetings to formulate for themselves the guiding principles of a philosophy of education that reaches clearly into all the practices of the school and the additional courage and intelligence to apply this thinking to making such changes as seem necessary in any of the school's practices. (W. A. Robinson, 1937) |
| Addressing the Needs of Black Students | We must learn that the main responsibility of the secondary school is to condition the young Negro for changes in American economic life. (Harold L. Trigg, 1935) |
| Generating Caring Relationships with Students | Somehow the teacher has to get across this barrier and this means establishing a relationship with the individual, because the best hope for stimulating the desire is that this student will identify himself with you or with some teacher. (Allison Davis, 1958) |

children. "We know, don't we?" the president said as he ended his lecture, inferring that they as Black educators understood the difficulties facing their students and also understood how to help the students overcome those difficulties. "We must be the agents of what we know." He ended his speech with resounding affirmation from listeners.

The commitment to meeting the needs of Black children was also evidenced in the poem fellows read that had been written by a Black principal of a formerly segregated school. Reflecting upon his commitment to children, Ulysses Byas wrote:

OUR RESPONSIBILITY AS A PUBLIC SCHOOL DISTRICT IS TO
EDUCATE ALL CHILDREN
CHILDREN FROM TWO PARENT HOMES, ONE PARENT HOMES, OR THOSE
CHILDREN FROM HOMES WITH NO PARENT AT ALL

CHILDREN FROM SPACIOUS, EXPENSIVE HOMES;
OR CRAMPED, DILAPIDATED HOMES.

CHILDREN FROM MORTGAGED HOMES, RENTED HOMES, WELFARE HOMES,
FOSTER HOMES OR ORPHANAGE HOMES. CHILDREN FROM CARING HOMES,
SHARING HOMES, SUPPORTIVE HOMES, SELFISH HOMES OR ENVIOUS
HOMES. CHILDREN FROM EDUCATIONALLY CHEATED HOMES, HOMES
WITH
UNEMPLOYMENT AND/OR UNDEREMPLOYMENT

CHILDREN FROM EDUCATED HOMES, LOVING HOMES, GOOD HOMES;
ILLITERATE HOMES, LONELY HOMES, BROKEN HOMES
OR CHILDREN FROM NO HOME AT ALL.

CHILDREN! COME! SHORT OR TALL, THIN OR PLUMP, DISADVANTAGED OR
GIFTED, PLAIN OR HANDSOME, SPECIAL OR NORMAL, DRAMATIC OR
ATHLETIC, POETIC OR MUSICAL. CHILDREN! COME! WILLIFUL OR
FORCED, STUDIOUS OR LAZY, INTELLIGENT OR DULL, QUESTFUL OR
QUESTLESS, FORCEFUL OR SHY, LAWFUL OR LAW-BREAKER.
IT REALLY MAKES NO DIFFERENCE! COME! [1]

The fellows discussed Mr. Byas's words and reflected on their commitments to the students they served. In many ways, their commitments mirrored their predecessors'.

Finally, fellows discussed the "trickster" motif historically utilized by Black principals when school boards remained unresponsive to the needs of their schools. The university representative provided two case studies of problems faced by a Black principal and invited fellows to speculate collaboratively on ways they would solve the problems. Amidst laughter, the group soon discovered that the need to "trick" boards and other school leaders remained essential to addressing the real needs in their urban schools.

At the end of the first professional development session for TITUS, fellows had delved into the history of Black principals in professional meetings, engaging in shared commitments with each other. They discovered the problems that confronted them in educating urban children were not unlike the problems confronted by Black principals in previous decades. They also learned that their values about how schools should be run and how they might problem-solve were not unlike those principals of earlier years.

For the fellows, session one placed their current activities within a historical context. At its conclusion, the university representative asked fellows to bring one or two parents with them to the next professional development meeting.

## Session 2: Teachers and Parental Involvement

During the second workshop session, the university representative sought to help fellows and active parents from their schools understand the historical ways Black parents and principals worked together. The parents the fellows brought watched a film depicting the support of Black parents for Black schools historically. The fellows listened to a lecture from the university representative about Black parental support in the segregated era and received a number of handouts related to the history they were being exposed to.

The handouts depicted forms of Black parental involvement from the National Colored PTA, through regional meetings, and finally to a song sung at PTA meetings. The principals and parents met separately so that principals could learn about the history but not be placed in the awkward position of learning it at the same time as the parents. Although the format of presentation differed for the different session participants, all learned about the centrality of "key" people who could function as school advocates, as well as the ways Black principals of another era intentionally courted the support of parents through presence in the community, language patterns, and school events.

At the end of the session's learning modules, fellows and parents reconvened to discuss perceptions of relationships between current urban school parents and principals. The conversation was rich as each group depicted how it saw the other. Charts were drawn, ideas debated, and strategies considered. Independent of the university representative's planned third session on teachers and professional development, the fellows and the parents decided to continue their talk, discussing how to court and sustain parental support.

## Session 3: School and Communities—Where Do We Go from Here?

Despite the representatives' original plans for session three, fellows reconvened with some parents from the previous session to continue their conversations about generating school involvement among contemporary urban parents. Despite attempts by the school representative to facilitate the workshop, the conversations needed little steering, as the fellows and parents continued to strategize together about ways to create additional parental involvement.

The summer workshops were the first of several meetings with fellows on the university campus. At their conclusion, all agreed that the collaborative time together allowed fellows to understand more fully the historical model of African American education they embodied while also building professional relationships with each other and with the university. They particularly affirmed the principals' desire for a safe haven, free from reproach, reprimand, censure, or reprisal. They appreciated the opportunity to exchange ideas with colleagues sharing similar challenges. When together, they appeared to visibly exhale. One commented: "We have no place where we can talk freely." In the current educational climate, she said, "no one dares speak out."[2]

Because of the summer workshops, authentic relationships between the university representative, the school representative, and the fellows solidified. With the vision of the African American Pedagogical Model clearly articulated, the fellows now committed themselves to working with the university to replicate the model where possible. Together, the university representative, the school representative, and the fellows discussed logistics for the remainder of the year. The next step in the process was to identify areas of need where fellows believed their schools could use university support and to build a team of university stakeholders who could deliver those needs, despite limited people and almost nonexistent financial resources. For this phase of the project, the support of a TITUS team was essential.

### IDEAS TO CONSIDER

- Plan professional development spaces that allow university and school leaders to feel comfortable exchanging ideas.
- Give fellows decision-making power to determine their "safe space" for professional collaboration.
- Send nonverbal messages to principals that communicate respect for their leadership, inclusive of interactions with school staff and preparation for the meetings, materials, and site.
- Provide intellectual opportunities for the principals to learn about the African American Pedagogical Model.

- Carefully plan the format of engagement with the model, including visuals, handouts, PowerPoint, film, case studies, and so on, but create opportunities for autonomy if the fellows collaboratively decide on another topic or the need for another topic arises.
- Ensure that some of the attributes of principals selected include a commitment to children, a willingness to give them the best, and a desire to track children as well as all people in the educational environment when necessary to be sure that children get what they need.
- Is the principal allowed to bring school personnel into a professional learning space, and is the university leader willing to allow principals to function as authorities in the shared spaces?
- Is there evidence that the principals begin to "own" the sessions?
- Do principals speak positively of the exchange, unsolicited?

## NOTES

1. Unpublished Ulysses Byas papers, MARBL Collection, Emory University.
2. Author's field notes, June 10, 2012.

*Chapter Three*

# Creating TITUS Buy-In Among Various Stakeholders

## Tiffany D. Pogue and Amber Jones

To function in alignment with the historical model, Teaching in the Urban South (TITUS) needed more than the commitment of principals, the leadership of the university, and the school representatives. It also needed (1) a group of doctoral students committed to the goals of the historical model and the possibility for contemporary replication; (2) a cadre of students and volunteers to help facilitate deliverables and events; (3) other committed educators; and (4) an engaged community.

This chapter outlines the processes by which the TITUS team was able to generate student and stakeholder buy-in and commitment to its version of the historical model.

### SHARED VISIONS, BELIEFS, AND COMMITMENTS AMONG TITUS TEAM MEMBERS

At the same time the school and university representatives were working toward building camaraderie with the fellows, relationships with the doctoral students who would be charged with much of the TITUS work were also underway. The students who would form the core of the TITUS team first collectively envisioned the project when the vision for the TITUS initiative was introduced to departmental faculty, staff, and students. At a DES professional seminar, the university representative helped faculty, staff, and students understand how the historical model could be linked to the mission of the division. Specifically, the university representative drew on the verbiage of the DES mission statement—"to reform and improve education, particularly urban education"—in order to make plain the connections between the rhetoric of the division and the responsibilities embedded within the TITUS vision.

After the introductory statement, students used small-group discussions to imagine how being "actively involved in schools and other educational institutions in the community" overlapped with their own commitments and coursework in urban education.[1] Although the university representative expressed concern at the end of the conversations regarding the amount of time and sacrifice doctoral students would have to give to launch the initiative, the response of one doctoral student captured the sentiment of many: "We want to be able to tell our children that when there was a battle to fight, we fought."

Importantly, the DES students who joined the initiative already shared certain values and commitments that generated immediate interest in the project. Through coursework and prior experiences, DES doctoral students interested in TITUS shared similar beliefs and values. These included:

- exposure to the African American Pedagogical Model's belief in, and desire to help, urban students;
- identification with the children in surrounding local schools; and
- affiliation with the community being served.

## Exposure to the Historical Model

All of the TITUS team members were DES doctoral students and visiting scholars who had been exposed to the historical model prior to their involvement with the initiative. Some of the doctoral students were exposed to the model through coursework. This coursework had highlighted historical attempts to provide quality education to all students equally and had provided examples of ways individuals operating in the community had always been able to overcome obstacles to their efforts, even if on a small scale. Other doctoral students had guardians or parents who had attended segregated schools and had passed down stories of their experiences.

Two students had personally attended segregated schools, one during the years of de jure segregation and the other during de facto segregation in urban schools; yet another member had data on the historical model generated by an individual research project. As a result of these prior experiences, each doctoral student entered the project with beliefs formed either by their own experiences or through coursework.

Joining with the team of doctoral students were two visiting scholars from other universities. These scholars had been exposed to TITUS through conversations with the university representative at professional meetings, like those held by the American Educational Research Association (AERA). Because of their shared experiences and vision, the visiting scholars elected to use their university sabbaticals to become part of the TITUS initiative. To-gether with the doctoral students, the visiting scholars helped comprise a team who understood the potential power of the historical model.

## A Belief in and Desire to Help Urban Students

The doctoral students also shared a mutual desire to serve urban students. The graduate students imagined a better future for students from marginal-ized populations. In imagining this better future, many had previously in-volved themselves in activities to support the educational experiences of urban youth. The doctoral students also understood that the educational op-portunities they had received improved their academic and social standings. As a result, this group of students possessed a shared commitment and was eager to use TITUS as a means to provide similar opportunities to other urban children.

Visiting scholars joining the TITUS team shared this commitment to serve urban youth. One of the visiting scholars commented that she was attracted to the notion that TITUS was a "concept of community with higher education acting as advocates for the community."[2]

## Identification with the Children in Surrounding Local Schools

All TITUS team members also identified with the students the TITUS initia-tive sought to impact. Specifically, the TITUS team shared many ethnic, racial, and socioeconomic realities of the students in local schools. They could see themselves in the faces of urban students. As a result, TITUS team members reported feeling responsible for supporting the educational experi-ences of students in much the same way that others had supported their own.

## Affiliation with the Community Being Served

Each of the TITUS team members previously lived in, taught in, and/or served as administrators in urban communities. These prior experiences in urban schools supported existing beliefs about urban students. Together, the team members created a unique sharing of experiences that made the TITUS team different from the university. As one TITUS team member reported, "I identify more closely with the community we serve and with the Division of Educational Studies than I do with Emory."[3] In sum, the TITUS team firmly believed that, even without substantial funding, it was entirely possible to disrupt the narratives of cultural deficit and perceived pathologies surround-ing urban students. These shared beliefs and commitments forged a team with multiple members but a single agenda. However, crafting this shared agenda happened in very specific ways as described throughout this book.

## INTENTIONED EFFORTS TO CREATE A COLLABORATIVE

The intentionality of TITUS became a crucial factor in attracting both doctoral students and outside faculty. Using the historical model as a foundation, the university representative wanted to move TITUS beyond research to operationalize and implement in real time the researched historical precepts. A degree of student buy-in already existed that had helped build the TITUS initiative. Beyond these preexisting dispositions, however, a major reason for the students' commitments to the TITUS initiative was an urgent desire to not only research the students in these settings but move beyond research to action that could make a difference in the lives of urban students.

## CREATING THE TITUS COMMUNITY

Recalling that the historical model included educators' insistence that the whole child be educated, the TITUS initiative insisted that the whole doctoral student—including their prior professional and organizational experiences—be resourced during its implementation. Working with TITUS meant that traditional educational hierarchies were leveled, and that faculty and students would work as educational partners.

### Mutual Ownership

Part of the willingness of doctoral students to sacrifice time and energy far exceeding course credit offered was due to a sense of mutual ownership in the conception and implementation of the TITUS initiative. All members of the TITUS team were allowed—and encouraged—to bring their full professional selves to the initiative in ways they had seldom experienced in their roles as doctoral students. Before the TITUS initiative, the identity of "student" was firmly established *for* these individuals after they had been accepted into the graduate program at Emory. However, once the initiative began, the identity of "student" took on a more nuanced manifestation as "professional with previous experiences" who happened to be in the role of student.

   For example, the school representative responsible for engaging community partners drew on her past professional experiences and relationships as the team planned interactions with schools. Other team members drew on knowledge of public relations and corporate experiences, or experiences as classroom teachers. Instead of leading conversations with these students, the university representative listened. Eventually the university representative admitted that the TITUS initiative allowed her to see doctoral students as significant collaborators with professional identities outside of their roles as doctoral students. This shared professionalism disrupted traditional interactions between faculty and students and helped create mutual ownership, resulting in a subjective conceptualization of themselves as "the TITUS team." One example of how this mutual ownership operated was the creation of a logo for the initiative.

The newly formed TITUS team decided that it was necessary to create a logo that adequately represented the TITUS mission and the historical model. To keep costs manageable, rather than relying on a graphic artist, a TITUS team member created several drafts and brought them to a planning meeting. After reviewing the drafts, the team collectively decided that the proposed images failed to promote a professional image and failed to convey TITUS's commitment to urban schools and students. Recognizing the need for a more professional representation, the team elected to find someone who would be willing to provide their professional services pro bono.

With a decision to draw on community resources, the team approached a member's spouse, an experienced graphic artist and photographer. This community stakeholder generated several sample logos that the team reviewed before selecting the present logo for TITUS. The current logo features an open window in a classroom overlooking an urban landscape that represented the community TITUS sought to serve. To TITUS team members, the logo spoke to the wide-open opportunities that could be presented to urban school students as a result of TITUS efforts. Next to this image is the TITUS acronym and full name, "Teaching in the Urban South." Finally, the image contains, in its bottom right corner, a check mark representing the shared governance of TITUS members. Because of its symbolic value, this logo eventually became a standard feature on TITUS flyers, conference programs, and social media. Its continued use is a testament to the power of collective effort and to the kinds of creative strategies that were necessary to overcome a lack of financial resources.

## Camaraderie During TITUS Meetings

The TITUS meetings were an essential and unique element of TITUS's implementation and success. Importantly, the meetings were purposeful, organized, and infused with collegial camaraderie. One of the visiting scholars described the meetings thus:

> The most prominent aspect of the meeting to me was the warm feeling of acceptance of everyone and of the gifts they brought to the group. This aspect was priceless, as students, professors, school workers, and community members were equally accepted and appreciated. I appreciated that in a room full of brilliant scholars, no one was made to feel any less brilliant.
>
> The next aspect that I appreciated was the order that was evident in every meeting. Meetings were semi-structured and very productive. I described the meetings as semi-structured because although there was always an agenda and

goals, meetings were not so structured that they did not leave time for good humor and laughter. As a group, TITUS students, volunteers, and faculty members appeared to be very happy to be part of the endeavor and to enjoy their various roles.

As noted by the team member who was a visiting scholar, the successful implementation of TITUS required acknowledgment of all team members' talents, expertise, and contributions. In this way, the TITUS meetings helped to create a collegial camaraderie.

However, community creation also included social interactions. A consistent element of TITUS planning meetings, like those in which the logo was generated, was the sharing of food. In the initial weekly meetings, team members decided that the early evening timing of the meetings meant food was required. Team members assigned partner groups to prepare dinner, and dinner soon became the transition between a day as a scholar and an evening as a researcher becoming a school advocate. Teams began to compete with one another to create new dishes, and the aroma of good food joined laughter and smiles at the beginning of every TITUS meeting.

Ask any TITUS team member about "TITUS chicken," and the member will sing the praises of Dr. Bass's wonderful self-generated recipe. A member might also mention Miyoshi's bean dip or Tirza's chicken salad as meeting staples. Once during a casual dinner held in a team member's home, core team members found themselves crowded around a kitchen table discussing plans for the following year. Though no one had planned for this social gathering, the meeting turned into a blend of work and laughter. It exemplified the visiting scholar's statement: TITUS meetings always included food and fellowship in addition to the obvious focus on work and achievement.

## Intragroup Accountability

Authentic relationships between the doctoral students and other members of the TITUS team formed a foundation for intragroup accountability that always held members in check and kept individuals on task. As the team began to create logos, websites, and other preparatory materials, no one wanted to report to his or her peers that an assigned task had remained undone or that complete effort had not been given toward a previously communicated goal. This group accountability was central to implementing the planning and delivery of the project.

TITUS members were also not afraid to offer constructive criticism to others, and members of the team did not feel uncomfortable sharing their ideas for, and critiques of, TITUS efforts. As a result, team members sought to earn respect from their peers by diligently working toward TITUS goals.

Each member reported the desire to maintain their peers' respect in a way that produced intragroup accountability.

## IDEAS TO CONSIDER

- Do you have a group of students who share a belief in, and desire to assist, urban students?
- Do you have a way to familiarize potential student participants with the historical model?
- Do you have students who have previous experiences in urban schools?
- Is the department prepared to host an open conversation aligning its commitments with TITUS activities?
- Are students given the opportunity to generate ownership in the project?
- Are meetings settings of professional collaboration?
- Are meetings community-building?
- Do team members elicit high standards and accountability from one another?

## NOTES

1. The Division of Educational Studies, (n.d.). Mission statement. Retrieved from http://des.emory.edu/home/.
2. Peterson, personal interview with author, 2015.
3. Personal interview with author, April 19, 2013.

*Chapter Four*

# Focus on
# Problem-Solving and Deliverables

## Brandi Hinnant-Crawford and Miyoshi Juergensen

Prior to the beginning of the school year and during the TITUS team's first official year, the university representative and the school representative returned to the schools of each of the fellows to confirm with them the specific needs they believed the TITUS team could help address in their schools. Although the summer conversations had revealed broad areas of need for all schools, the intent of the university representative and the school representative in this final round of school visits was to be sure each fellow had the opportunity to identify the particular needs for his or her school. TITUS wanted to address individually specified needs, not the compilation of collective needs.

Because of the summer engagement, conversations with the fellows flowed smoothly and easily. Fellows talked, thoughtfully responding to the question of need, while the university representative and school representative took notes and asked additional priming questions designed to encourage the fellows to elaborate. When the university and school representatives compiled a list after meeting with each fellow, needs included developing college preparation activities, creating additional programs and documents, and increasing parental involvement. The particular requests within each category were so expansive that, when the university representative first presented the list to the faculty during its fall retreat, university faculty members stared wide-eyed, unbelieving that the TITUS team could fulfill the needs requested. Surely TITUS would have to limit its deliverables, many thought. The TITUS team, however, responded differently to the list.

The TITUS team held its first meeting in the fall and examined the list carefully. The team convening around the conference room table that had previously hosted the fellows consisted of the doctoral students, who were committed to the TITUS model from earlier meetings and classes. They had built trust in one another to fulfill responsibilities. They shared a commitment to urban schools, and they interacted easily with both the university representative and the school representative. This team examined the list of school needs and began creating a structure to deliver on school requests.

This chapter describes the liaison model the TITUS team formulated to address the problems fellows presented. Like the fellows and similar to the historical model, the issue they tackled was how to *solve the problems* in urban schools. In this chapter, the process of preparing TITUS team members to enter the schools, the process for delivering needs, and the critical elements that facilitated relationships are addressed.

## INTRODUCING LIAISONS

Although fellows were comfortable with the university representative and the school representative, once the business of the school year began, each fellow needed a contact person to facilitate ongoing communication with the TITUS team. At its fall meeting, the TITUS team discussed the relationships that often existed between public schools and universities. Because the team did not assume that successful summer engagement guaranteed a successful series of interactions throughout the school year, they decided that each fellow needed a TITUS team member with whom they could engage continuously throughout the school year and whom they could trust to oversee the deliverables in their school.

The assignment of a team–fellow liaison happened intentionally. After discussing the personalities and interests of each fellow, the TITUS team matched their interests with the interests of fellows. The goal was to create a good "fit" with each fellow as a context for working together. The team collectively created assignments based on such characteristics as communication patterns, similarity of college or community organizations, and mutual interests. After a liaison had been named for each fellow, the team practiced ways of introducing themselves to the fellows so that the relationships created by the school and university representatives during the summer could be extended.

In a full evening's meeting, the school representative, herself a former principal, discussed with team members how to enter school places respectfully. She led them in strategies for addressing secretaries in their opening visit, methods for expressing their concern for the time constraints under which fellows operated, and means by which to talk with the school leaders that demonstrated respect for them as professional colleagues. Although the members of the team were doctoral students, the school representative's goal was to minimize hierarchy in favor of collaboration, and much of the minimization could be addressed through intentioned forms of language and demeanor. Amidst laughter and many questions, the school representative rehearsed first school visits with team members through simulation and role play.

The first planned school visit for TITUS team members would also involve conveying important information to the fellows. The liaison was expected to discuss deliverables for the school and provide fellows with information on TITUS-planned events throughout the year. In preparation for this first visit, the team prepared identical "fellow packets" each liaison would carry. The packet included a letter the university representative intended for the school superintendent, describing each fellow's participation in TITUS during the summer and including lists of readings, services, workshops, and upcoming events.

The team discussed in detail how to present the superintendent letter to the fellows. They discussed the need to affirm trust between themselves and the fellows by making sure the language to the superintendent conveyed shared beliefs about appropriate information to share. To communicate this concern to the fellows, the team scripted for one another the conversations they expected to have with the fellows. The conversation script noted the following:

> We don't want anything to go to the superintendent without you approving it first. If you have any concerns about it, please call me [the liaison] and let me know. If you have any big questions/concerns you can call Sheryl [the school representative] or Dr. V. S. W. [the university representative]. . . . We wanted to put together a letter that is really honoring you.

The team also discussed how to present the other items in the folder and how to ready themselves for the meeting. The talking points on which they agreed included the following:

- Photocopy your folder before you go so that you can have one to flip through when they're reading.
- Emphasize each principal's position as a fellow.
- Refer to V. S. W.'s cell phone number if they need to follow up on who we are.
- Remind them of the Noguera chapter in their blue folders.[1]
- Sell the TITUS idea and the workshops.
- Advertise the Noguera lecture and mixer. Noguera lecture and networking reception held for TITUS Fellows, the TITUS team, and friends of the initiative.
- Discuss the vision for the TITUS spring conference.

Although being coached on language and presentation suggests a lack of authenticity in the individual relationships the team expected the liaison and the fellow to create, the school and university representatives believed a conversational map allowed liaisons to engage fellows in ways that would lead to authentic relationships, while also building on relationships built during the summer. The school liaisons would provide a critical link between the schools and the team, and the team wanted uniformity in delivery for all fellows. See figure 4.1 for a conceptual representation of the relationships between the actors during TITUS implementation.

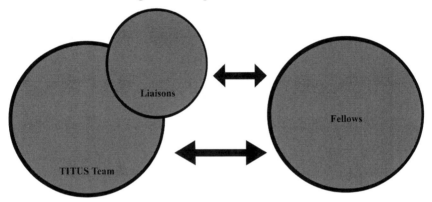

**Figure 4.1.   Relationship among TITUS actors. Courtesy of TITUS Team Archives**

Following preparation for the first visits, liaisons maintained their own independent, ongoing relationships with fellows. In these interactions, they noted the concerns and questions of the fellows and communicated these queries back to the TITUS team. They also conveyed information from the team to the fellows. The sample email below illustrates the ongoing communication that took place between fellows and their liaisons. In this example, the liaison was Miyoshi Juergensen. The bold print represents the fellow's responses to the liaison.

> Miyoshi,
> **Good morning. The answers to your questions are listed below in bold:**
> I hope this email finds you well since our meeting. Per our discussion, I talked with our team about the ways in which you'd like us to assist you regarding increased graduation and AP/IB test scores. We are still working on the logistics of the workshop for graduation coaches. I expect to have something more definitive to you by the end of the month. In the interim, can you provide your graduation coach's contact information?
> **Graduation coach: K. Johnson, XXX-XXX-XXXX or XXX-XXX-XXXX**
> I would like to open the lines of communication if that is alright with you. Regarding your concerns about your AP/IB test scores, we have a team mem-

ber who is really excited about working with you and your teachers on this. Her name is Dr. Lisa Bass, and she is a visiting professor in our department working exclusively with TITUS in areas such as these. I have attached her CV for your convenience. She'd like to first talk with you a bit about the programs. I can put her in contact with you as soon as you give the green light :).

**I'm looking forward to working with Dr. Lisa Bass. Please feel free to move forward with providing my contact information. Thanks so much.**

In a less monitored role, liaisons also worked to identify resources in each school community and convey this information to fellows. They looked for major businesses, civic organizations, and religious institutions surrounding the school that could support education within the school. Their goal was to create a bank of resources that could be used as a database for fellows and staff in their schools.

On the role of the liaison in the TITUS project, fellow Greg Goodwin reflected: "My interaction with my liaison was incredible. . . . I could always communicate via email and phone calls." Fellow Pam Benford agreed: "Someone was always accessible to work with me on concerns unique to my school." In sum, the liaison provided each fellow an easily accessible TITUS representative. "It was extremely convenient," added fellow Goodwin.

## SERVICES DELIVERED

After the liaisons introduced themselves to fellows, established protocols for communication, and affirmed the tentative list of school needs, the team began to strategize on ways to provide the support each fellow requested. They were gratified to see that all requests reflected the fellows' common commitment to the development of their students. They also commented on the level of trust each fellow exhibited in allowing him- or herself to be viewed as vulnerable by articulating areas of needed support. The team then began the serious work of figuring out how to harness the breadth and depth of expertise around the table and use it to address the articulated needs.

The team began by forming a series of committees to address a collapsed set of needs. They needed to decide which of them had the best expertise to perform different services and the method of delivery for each of the services. To do so, the team carefully reviewed the list of needed services and then discussed who could support each need using an informal internal assessment.

While sitting around the table examining the needs and desires of the fellows, the question was raised, "Who can do what?" It was in this moment that inner-team trust was most consequential. Members had to trust that other members could perform the stated tasks. Their familiarity with each other's backgrounds and skill sets aided in their ability to trust each other to perform the designated services.

The team quickly recognized that not all services could be provided by existing team members. The conversation broadened to identify other potential service providers, such as those in team members' personal networks. The team pondered possible partnerships with other organizations on campus. They reflected on potential businesses that might supply materials. Each team member then assumed the responsibility of making connections with another person or organization as needed to complete a delivery plan.

At the end of the conversation, the team developed a chart to document intended activities throughout the year (see table 4.1).

**Table 4.1.**

| Services | TITUS Team Member Qualifications | Service Medium |
|---|---|---|
| College entrance exam preparation | College Board tutor | Workshop |
| Data mining | Educational and professional experiences with standardized tests and item analysis; aligned research agenda | Fact sheet (see appendix A) |
| Math tutoring | Emory graduate students in math and science departments | Assigned to external volunteers |
| Professional development | Knowledge of HAAPN and its implementation | Noguera lecture; spring conference |
| Graduation support | Former teacher at a school for students at risk; aligned research agenda | Workshop |
| College essay writing | Former high school English Language Arts (ELA) teacher | Workshop |
| Increased parental support | Experience with nonprofit community-building projects | Noguera lecture; spring conference |
| Developing Black history program | Former high school ELA teacher | School-wide assembly |
| Historiography of school | Served on archival research team | Yearbook |
| Initiative for Black male youth | Aligned research agenda | Fact sheet |

Importantly, TITUS planned delivery of the services above without an operating budget. Instead, the team utilized the assets and networks present within the room, the department, and the university. Much like during the historical moment in which the African American Pedagogical Model existed, the human and social capital of the team funded TITUS.

## Delivery and Communication

Clear, accurate, and timely communication was the foundation of successful service delivery. Liaisons invited all fellows back to Emory for a meeting with the full TITUS team. At the meeting, the team presented a buffet of anticipated services. Some of the services related to the individual requests of a fellow for his or her school. Some of the services could be collapsed and delivered across schools.

Fellows reviewed the list, asking questions as necessary, and then began to volunteer to host particular events at their schools and suggest optimal dates for the events to occur across school communities. The interactions that delivered the college entrance exam workshop and the essay-writing workshop are noted here. Based on the expertise of specific team members, the SAT workshop was one of the first TITUS events held for students. After the joint meeting, a team member sent an initial email regarding the event:

> Greetings TITUS Principals,
>
> I thoroughly enjoyed meeting with you all yesterday. Thank you so much for allowing the Division of Educational Studies to be a part of your school communities. I would also like to extend my gratitude to Mr. Goodwin for volunteering his school as the location for the SAT workshop. As promised, attached is the information sheet regarding the SAT preparation workshop. Feel free to email me or call me with any questions.
>
> Thank you,
> Brandi

After providing registration information and event flyers to all the fellows, the communication narrowed to the hosting principal, that school's liaison, and the particular team member in charge of the event.

## IDEAS TO CONSIDER

- Does the school identify its needs from the university, rather than the university assuming its capacity to meet needs it identified?
- Does the university team focus on providing support for the problems identified by the principals?
- Is a team member assigned to each school leader?
- Are the team members rehearsed in communication and cultural norms before they go to the school?

- Is a comfortable, ongoing mode of communication established between the university and school?
- Is the university intentional about creating support that draws on the expertise of university personnel?

## NOTE

1. Because Pedro Noguera, a nationally known and well-respected scholar of urban education, was the featured speaker during the conference, the TITUS team wanted to share some of his work with the Fellows.

*Chapter Five*

# Professional Development and Community Engagement

## Latrise Johnson

Formalizing and creating brand recognition for TITUS as a unique entity was essential to garnering maximum community interest, support, and participation for TITUS events. To reach the maximum number of participants, the team created and used social media content to promote community engagement.

The TITUS team and fellows also realized that alignment with the historical model required planning and implementation of collaborative, multidirectional professional development. This alignment entailed bringing teachers, parents, students, community members, and higher education professionals together in collaborative spaces to engage in problem-posing and problem-solving around urban educational issues. The TITUS team designed and offered collaborative professional development in two settings: one university-sponsored event and two school-based conferences. Each of these professional development and community engagement opportunities were fostered and guided by:

- creation and use of media for community exposure,
- use of collaborative spaces and places,
- the Noguera lecture (an example of community engagement),
- a first school-based conference, and
- a second school-based conference.

CREATION AND USE OF MEDIA FOR COMMUNITY EXPOSURE

As an initial step in getting the word out about TITUS and its planned professional development, the TITUS team realized that advertisement would be essential. To ensure maximum media coverage and community exposure for optimal stakeholder recognition and participation, the team created a TITUS logo (as described in chapter 4), used social media, created flyers and press releases, and participated in community outreach events.

## Use of Social Media

The TITUS team believed that outreach through social media was the most cost-effective means of creating community exposure. To achieve this goal, the team decided to create social media accounts on Tumblr, Twitter, and Facebook. The team also created a WordPress account that served as a space to describe the TITUS mission, feature profiles of TITUS fellows, and publicize TITUS events. The Division of Educational Studies (DES) website was updated to include a link to this WordPress blog.

The Tumblr and Twitter accounts were seldom used, but the TITUS Facebook page featured photographs of TITUS events, a brief description of the TITUS initiative, and status updates that addressed upcoming TITUS events and other issues relevant to urban schooling. Although a single team member was responsible for updating these social media accounts, all team members had an equal say in what would be posted and when. In addition to social media, the team also relied on more traditional means of publicity.

## Use of Flyers and Press Releases

For every event, the TITUS team created a flyer. These flyers included a description of the event, the TITUS logo, and the date and time of the function. Because TITUS initially operated under the auspices of the DES, the Emory University name also usually appeared on publicity materials. The decision to include the Emory name was based on a shared understanding that the name carried cachet in the local area.

### Flyers

Flyers were usually designed, copied, and disseminated by TITUS doctoral students. Members rotated flyer design responsibilities but ensured that the entire team vetted a design before copies were made. In a few cases, a single flyer would be taken to a counselor at a fellow's school so that copies could be made and disseminated within the building. Flyers were posted throughout the university community, in various buildings and meeting spaces, to disseminate information regarding TITUS activities on campus. In schools, flyers would occasionally be sent home with students. (See figure 5.1 for an example.)

*Press Releases*

The university representative worked with an Emory faculty member outside of the DES to fashion a press release that would generate additional buzz around the pilot-year Noguera Conference. The press release was vetted before its release, during a TITUS team meeting, and was later sent out to local and campus media outlets. While it cannot yet be determined if the flyers were more effective than the press release, it can be noted that only one press release was created during the first two years of TITUS's implementation, while flyers and social media were used throughout.

## Participation in Community Outreach Efforts

The TITUS team also used events within school communities to engage the community and generate interest in TITUS. The TITUS team understood that to engage the community, they would have to go into the community and participate in outreach activities such as a "Back to School Forum for Parents," sponsored by a local church. During this event some TITUS team members set up a table with TITUS flyers and brochures, where team members shared information about TITUS and upcoming events. Others participated in the panel discussion about what parents needed to know about schools. One particularly poignant moment was the reading of an original poem by a student who was asked to participate in subsequent TITUS and community events. The by-product of the team's participation was increased community exposure and the establishment of nascent community ties. Ultimately, the use of various types of media introduced TITUS and TITUS events to the community writ large.

## Collaborative Spaces for Professional Development

To implement the model as accurately as possible, the team needed to plan collaborative professional development opportunities that (1) valued the voices of academics and practitioners equally, (2) allowed for multidirectional exchange of ideas, and (3) involved all community stakeholders, including students. By working collaboratively, the TITUS team and fellows developed programming open to the academic and K–12 community. Because this programming was designed to equally engage stakeholders in social and intellectual conversations, they honored a multidirectional flow of knowledge rather than a unidirectional flow of knowledge that privileged academia.

To this end, the team and the fellows determined to offer two professional development events during the pilot year. The first event, cosponsored by the

Saturday, April 21, 2012
8:30 am - 3:00 pm

Cedar Grove High School
2360 River Road
Ellenwood, Georgia 30294

# African American Excellence in Education:
## *Reclaiming the Past, Preparing for the Future*

An Education Conference hosted by Teaching in the Urban South

### Sessions to Include:

- **Using African American History in Teaching**
- **Current Trends in Math Education**
- **Inspiring Scientists for the Next Generation**
- **Literacy Practices In and Out of School**
- **Language Teaching: Current Challenges**
- **Gender-Based Education**
- **Preparing for the Principalship** (a special session for Assistant Principals)
- **Parental Involvement, Business Partnerships, and School Support**
- **High School to College: Pathways for Students and Parents**

**Figure 5.1.    Example of a flyer sent home with students. Courtesy of TITUS Team Archives**

Race and Difference Initiative (RDI), designed to "address the complexity of the human condition and human experience in a pluralistic, democratic society,"[1] featured Pedro Noguera and the TITUS fellows on a panel. The second school-based event was hosted by one of the fellows at her high school.

## THE NOGUERA LECTURE AS AN EXAMPLE OF COMMUNITY
## ENGAGEMENT AND MULTIDIRECTIONAL KNOWLEDGE FLOW

The first professional development exchange occurred during the Pedro Noguera lecture. TITUS team members chose the Pedro Noguera lecture as the springboard for informed and open dialogue open to all local stakeholders. In keeping with the historical model, the Noguera lecture involved considering how best to engage the community intellectually in problem-solving. Additionally, the Noguera lecture represented an opportunity to expand the educational discourse, which often excludes community voices. Pedro Noguera's popularity and focus on urban education made him an ideal candidate for the first TITUS-hosted conference.

### Intellectual and Community Engagement in a University Setting

The team realized that the key to bridging gaps that exist between the academy and schools, between schools and communities, and between educators and parents was to invite all stakeholders to participate—as valued, knowledgeable participants—in professional development opportunities. To ensure a wide variety of stakeholder presence and full participation, prior to the event, the team members reminded the fellows several times that they would serve as responders on a panel designed to "talk back" to Noguera.

The TITUS fellows in turn invited their teachers, students, and parents. Further, in the spirit of the event, and in response to growing competition among fellows to solicit attendees, fellow Mrs. Benford boasted that she was responsible for the presence of the largest contingency of students and parents. Other members of the TITUS team reached out to Emory's larger academic community through email and flyers. During meetings, TITUS team members also reached out to other local networks.

For example, one of the members reached out to the National Pan-Hellenic Council in order to invite interested members of the Greek-lettered community. The invitation was also extended to churches in the community, educators from other districts, and affiliates of numerous educational initiatives. All who were willing to engage in the open dialogue to "improve our nation's schools" were invited.

Finally, on the night of October 31, over two hundred scholars, practitioners, parents, students, and the university community at large crowded into the Jones Woodruff Room in Emory University's library to hear Noguera's formal lecture, titled "The Role of Research and the Politics of School Reform: Why We Don't Use What We Know to Improve Our Nation's Schools," which set the tone for the informed dialogue.

Immediately following Noguera's lecture, each TITUS fellow talked for three minutes on issues that were important to their respective school communities. At the end of the event, fellow Goodwin highlighted his feelings about having the space to engage with members of the community in informed dialogue, saying, "I had just considered myself just an ordinary principal, but associated with these folks, they make me feel like I am smart." Being able to talk about the issues of his school within a larger educational context, outlined during Noguera's lecture, illuminated how practitioners (namely, principals) and academics engaged in meaningful exchange in order to, according to fellow Amey, solve problems together.

## Engaging the Voices of Students in a University Setting

Following the historical model, the team realized that it was important to the event's success that students also have an opportunity to raise questions, make comments, voice concerns, and/or offer solutions to the issues in urban schools.

To prepare students to engage in meaningful conversation, one of the TITUS team members worked with a group of students to develop questions about their concerns related to their education. During the lecture, the students were invited to sit in the first row. After the lecture and during the Q& A session, many of the students responded to comments and ideas generated from the panel and posed their own questions and commentary about their educational experiences in urban schools. In addition, a student from a local performing arts academy recited a poem that illuminated many of the issues students in urban schools face.

Importantly, and in contrast to most other models of engagement, in which only one voice is dominant—that of the academic—this event provided opportunities for multiple voices.

## Reflections on the Noguera Lecture

The success of the Noguera lecture provided a clear understanding of the importance of the relationship between academics and practitioners, the role of community, and the honoring and centering of a multitude of voices. Empowered by the exchange, participants were in no hurry to leave.

The event also shaped the planning of the first TITUS spring conference by (1) demonstrating the capacity of the TITUS team to engage the community and higher education concurrently in professional development, (2) demonstrating the plausibility of hosting events with little to no material resources, and (3) bolstering the team's confidence in the community's interest in related events. By aligning the Noguera lecture with the historical model, the TITUS team fostered a climate of respect and centered the voices of members of the community in ways that conventional professional development could not.

Emory University Division of Educational Studies
&
Teaching In The Urban South (TITUS)
present

# PEDRO
# NOGUERA

Pedro Noguera is the Peter L. Agnew
Professor of Education in Steinhardt School of
Education at New York University. Noguera is
an urban sociologist whose scholarship and
research focuses on the ways in which schools
are influenced by social and economic
conditions in the urban environment.
Pedro Noguera has published over one
hundred research articles, monographs and
research reports on topics such as urban
school reform, conditions that promote
student achievement, youth violence, the
potential impact of school choice and
vouchers on urban public schools, and race
and ethnic relations in American society.

Please join us

## October 31, 2011
## 4:00 PM
## Jones Room, Level 3, Woodruff Library

Figure 5.2.    Flyer for the Noguera Lecture. Courtesy of TITUS Team Archives

PROFESSIONAL DEVELOPMENT CONTINUED:
TWO SCHOOL-BASED SPRING CONFERENCES

## 2012 Teaching in the Urban South (TITUS) Youth Achievement Award

Name: _____ School _____

Grade: _____ Teacher: _____

Address: _____ City: _____

State: _____ Zip: _____ Phone: _____

Email: _____

Gender: ☐Female ☐ Male

Race/Ethnicity

☐ African American/Black        ☐ Hispanic/Latino

☐ Asian/Pacific Islander        ☐ Native American/American Indian

☐ Caucasian/White               ☐ Other _____

How did you hear about the Teaching in the Urban South (TITUS) Youth Achievement Award? _____

**Please type your answers to the following questions and attach it to this cover sheet .**

1. List any activities that you have participated in at school or in your community (such as clubs, publications, drama, music, sports, etc.). If you have held any leadership roles in these activities, please describe as well.

2. Briefly describe your educational and/or career goals and your plans to achieve them.

3. In what ways do you believe youth can affect change in their communities and how education can assist in this change?

**Please return Applications by April 13, 2012.**

**Figure 5.6.   Example of TITUS award application. Courtesy of TITUS Team Archives**

Based on the understanding of the relationship between academics and practitioners, the role of the community, and the honoring and centering of a multitude of voices in the conversation outlined in the historical model, the TITUS team used the theme "Reclaiming the Model of African American

**About TITUS**

Teaching in the Urban South (TITUS) is a community-university partnership. TITUS aims to connect educational leaders in public schools with Emory scholars and students during summer learning opportunities and year-round events. We hope to create collaborative spaces for school-based inquiry where participants can engage in a dialogue and exchange of best practices.

**Contributors:**

The TITUS Team appreciates the generous support of Emory University's Division of Educational Studies, the Black Graduate Student Association at Emory University, the Emory University Race and Difference Initiative, Dr. Kharen Fulton, and the Nell Hodgson Woodruff School of Nursing (Arnita Howard and Dean Lynell A. Cadray)

**Thanks to:**

TITUS appreciates the attendance of DeKalb County School Board Members Mr. Bowen and Ms. Copelin-Wood. TITUS would also like to give special appreciation to our Fellows for their continued support and service to students:

Pamela Benford                Angelique Smith
Everett Patrick               Stephanie Amey
Greg Goodwin                  Thaddeus Dixon
Sheila Johnson Reese

Follow us on FACEBOOK at Teaching in the Urban South

Or visit our website: www.titusemory.wordpress.com

TITUS

TEACHING
IN
THE
URBAN
SOUTH

TITUS Presents:

**Reclaiming the African American Model for Excellence in Education:**
*Relationships Between Parents and Schools*

Cedar Grove High School
8:30 am – 3:00pm

**Figure 5.3.    Program for TITUS conference, outside. Courtesy of TITUS Team Archives**

Excellence in Education" for its first school-based spring conference. Convened at fellow Mrs. Benford's high school, Cedar Grove, the first spring conference was the culminating professional development event of TITUS's pilot year. Here, all members of the community—academics, teachers, fellows, parents, students, and other stakeholders—assembled for a day of social and intellectual engagement.

Reclaiming and replicating the historical delivery of professional development helped to guide and shape how the conference was planned. Additionally, it helped shape how the conference was delivered in the following ways:

- practitioners and scholars shared panels;
- students performed for their community and parents;
- communal meals were spaces for informal dialogue;
- community members, educators, and students were awarded for their excellence;
- societal issues related to race and discrimination were addressed; and

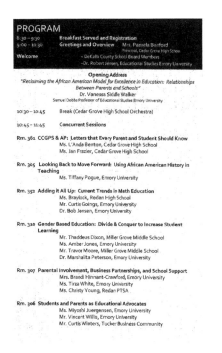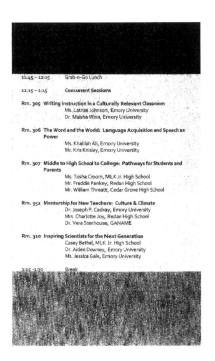

**Figure 5.4. Program for TITUS conference, inside. Courtesy of TITUS Team Archives**

- the keynote address explicitly described the historical African American Pedagogical Model.

## Planning a Conference Modeled from History: "Reclaiming the Model of African American Excellence in Education"

Planning for the spring conference involved close collaboration among the team and the fellows. As early as February 14, 2012, the TITUS team and fellows were invited to a planning meeting to determine a theme, purpose, and type of professional development that would be offered at the spring conference. During that meeting, a teacher-leader whom the hosting TITUS fellow identified as the point person/school liaison for the conference site also attended. At that time, the purpose as well as the theme of the conference was established. The theme would be "Reclaiming the Model of African American Excellence in Education." The purpose would be "to put people in conversation with one another about issues facing our students." Along with input from this school liaison, the TITUS fellows and team planned a conference "to-do" list that required "all hands on deck."

**Figure 5.5.    Participants at the TITUS conference. Courtesy of TITUS Team Archives**

Throughout the planning of the spring conference, the theme "Reclaiming the Model of African American Excellence in Education" guided decisions regarding the conference structure, outline, and delivery. For example, the conference involved (1) an opening address, (2) concurrent professional development sessions where practitioners and academics worked collaboratively to present cutting-edge research and practice, (3) meals, student entertainment, and awards that recognized two TITUS fellows who had made the most significant contribution to the overall TITUS effort during the pilot year, and (4) a town hall meeting in recognition of fellows and students.

Table 5.1 represents the multilayered responsibilities commensurate with planning a conference on this scale.

**Table 5.1.**

| Tasks | Person(s) Responsible | Tentative Date(s) | Date Completed /Confirmed |
|---|---|---|---|
| Confirm faculty involvement, Dr. Downey to send out info to undergraduates, Emory Admissions to follow-up, Slick to dean (with chair approval) | Dr. Siddle Walker | 4/10/2012 | |
| Contact churches | Dr. Siddle Walker, Latrise, Sheryl | 4/10/2012 | |

| Complete/review program, flyers, and registration | TITUS team & fellows | 4/10/2012 |
|---|---|---|
| Confirm speakers | TITUS team & fellows | 4/10/2012 |
| Report student entertainment | Brandi, Miyoshi | 4/10/2012 |
| Flyers, montage, signage | Latrise, Tiffany, Miyoshi | 4/10/2012 |
| Letter to board members | Sheryl | 4/3/2012 |
| Flyer distribution | Andrea | TBD |
| Food, sponsorship, library bags, recruit undergraduates, Karen Fulton | Vincent | 4/10/2012 |
| Food, confirm Black Graduate Student Association sponsorship, certificates, recruit undergraduates | Amber | 4/10/2012 |
| Press release and radio announcement | Tiffany | 4/10/2012 |
| Summer program brochures from the Atlanta University Center | Dr. Peterson | 4/10/2012 |
| Run-off packets | TITUS team | 4/17/2012 |
| Date to put packets together | TITUS team | 4/17–4/18/2012 |
| School readiness checklist/ walk-through | fellows, Dr. Siddle Walker, Sheryl, Brandi | 4/18–4/24/2012 |
| Room set-up | TITUS team, school personnel | TBD |
| Date to read and judge student entries | TBD | TBD |
| Monetary donations for student awards | Sheryl, Tiffany, Dr. Siddle Walker, Latrise, Vincent, Amber, Miyoshi | Discuss |

A day before the conference, one of the TITUS members sent this message that represented how the team understood what it meant to respect and honor the voices of others:

Fellow Conference Presenters,

I send you greetings on behalf of Dr. Siddle Walker and the TITUS team.
Tomorrow, educators will have the rare opportunity to stand alongside other stakeholders to engage in an exchange with one common goal—to im-

prove education for young people in our community. Practitioners, researchers, community leaders, students, and parents will discuss issues around access, testing, parental involvement, and current trends in education. I am honored to be among you as one of the facilitators of such important dialogue. I
am reminded that while I have conducted research, published, and presented in
certain areas, I must honor the voices of public school teachers, parents, students, and other individuals who may be present. I would encourage you to do
the same.

Let's remember that tomorrow is more about exchanging ideas and sus-
taining relationships than presenting ourselves as experts in particular fields of
study. In the spirit of tomorrow's conference, I look forward to "reclaiming the
past and preparing for the future."

Sincerely,
The TITUS Team

The email exemplified the tone of the conference as educators, parents, community members, and students joined to discuss issues that mattered to all of
them.

## Opening Session

The opening session of the spring conference featured an opening address
given by the university representative on the historical model and its significance for contemporary urban education. Designed to set the tone, explain
the purpose of the conference, and explain and stress the importance of the
model from which the conference derived, the opening address described the
historic relationship between schools and their communities and between
educators and parents, as well as the importance the historical model placed
on communities and schools working together to educate children. The university representative also explained that the name of the conference, "Reclaiming the Model of African American Excellence in Education," embodied an attempt to replicate aspects of the historical model.

## Planned Professional Development During the Conference

Using the historical model as a guide, the TITUS team collaborated to determine the type of professional development to deliver based on community-
identified needs. During the conference, paired scholars and practitioners led
content-specific, research-based sessions. Each session was designed to discuss strategies that worked in the four major disciplines: language arts, math,
science, and social studies. To address the needs of parents and community
members-at-large, the TITUS team enlisted the expertise of various community members, who led sessions for educators, parents, and students. The
conference also included sessions about parental involvement, current trends
in education, and college readiness.

## Communal Meals, Student Entertainment, and Awards

After the sessions, lunch was prepared and served by the cafeteria staff in the cafeteria of Cedar Grove. The room provided a space for continued dialogue and entertainment. In alignment with the historical model, students performed: the jazz band serenaded the conference attendees in the morning while the mixed chorus provided selections during lunch. Another aspect of the historical model was the bestowing of awards. Following lunch, two fellows, Benford and Goodwin, received awards and commendations for their work throughout the year. Students were also presented awards for the best student essays.

## Town Hall Session

The final phase of this first spring conference involved an open town hall session in which all present posed questions. The town hall meeting became the space specifically designed to engage parents in voicing their opinions on what they felt were the urgent needs of their children. The parents who participated in the conference—especially the town hall meeting—expressed excitement and discussed their desire for additional opportunities to participate in similar kinds of dialogue. TITUS fellows and the team believed that "when parents are well served, they are likely to be excited partners."

Evidence of their excitement, participation, and interest were demonstrated in the evaluations collected on that day. See appendix B for a summary of conference evaluations. Importantly, evaluations of the conference indicated that (1) the conference was "successful in recruiting the intended target population," (2) "respondents in general valued community–university partnership and the use of awards in educational improvement,"[2] (3) there were "high levels of instructional efficacy in individual sessions,"[3] and (4) participant responses suggested a high perception of the overall quality, efficacy, importance, and usefulness of the TITUS initiative and an increased interest in future participation and additional topics of discussion.[4] Overall, the evaluation indicated that the "organizers, contributors, and supporters were successful in achieving their goals and objectives."[5]

FROM THE KITCHEN TO THE CLASSROOM:
THE SECOND TITUS CONFERENCE

Buoyed by the success of the first TITUS conference, fellow Goodwin volunteered to host the second annual TITUS conference, themed "From the Kitchen to the Classroom," at his school. Even though both conferences were guided by the historical model, the second TITUS conference differed in significant ways from the first spring conference and provided valuable insights about the nature of TITUS and its mission.

## From the First to the Second Conference

From the completion of the first school-based conference to the planning stages for the second conference, several events occurred that threatened the second conference: (1) the announcement of the closing of the Division of Educational Studies; (2) the graduation of several founding team members; and (3) the school reassignment of some TITUS fellows. Even though the number of active TITUS fellows and TITUS team members dwindled, the remaining TITUS team and fellows continued to plan the second conference. While simultaneously working to complete their doctoral degrees, a handful of doctoral students assumed the reins to make the conference a reality.

The team could see that the first conference had an impact on the community. Throughout the planning of the second conference, people who attended the first conference and those who heard about TITUS continued to inquire about the upcoming conference.

At the same time, the school liaison designated by the principal of the host school demonstrated disinterest in the overall project. In contrast to the school liaison who assumed almost complete responsibility for the first conference, this new liaison designated assignments to others, missed deadlines, and generally left the organization of the conference to the principal. Ultimately, the principal and another designee worked with the TITUS team and continued the planning and execution of the conference. In spite of the principal's overflowing plate of responsibilities, he was determined to host the conference and ensure that it flowed smoothly.

Highlights of the second annual conference included:

- student participation;
- researcher/practitioner subject-area panels;
- a town hall discussion with parents about their students' needs; and
- student statements about their own schooling experiences and needs.

## Student Participation

From the beginning of the conference, students participated in various ways. During registration and lunch, the student jazz band serenaded conference attendees. For this conference, lunch was prepared and served by the school's award-winning Culinary Arts Department. Furthermore, during the town hall session, students prepared statements and asked questions of panel members about issues affecting their education.

## Researcher/Practitioner Subject-Area Panels

During concurrent conference sessions, practitioners and academics once again collaborated to present cutting-edge research in partnership with one another. Teachers and researchers served on panels that covered issues related to school leadership, parental involvement, pedagogical strategies, and more.

## Town Hall Session

The focal point of the second annual conference was the town hall session, which focused on problems plaguing urban communities and schools. Dr. Pearlie Dove, then ninety-two and a former professor of education at Clark College (Atlanta, GA), discussed some of the differences in pedagogy between the historical and contemporary models of teaching. She emphasized the "care ethic" of teachers under the historical model. It was also during the town hall session that panel participants discussed broader sociopolitical realities facing urban youth including, but not limited to, sex trafficking, parental obligations, school policies that frequently forced students out of schools, and the plight of African American males. Parents and community members in attendance were interested and asked for more information. The conference hosted over one hundred attendees, and at its end, one participant stated, "Even if TITUS doesn't do anything else, it needs to at least do this."

### IDEAS TO CONSIDER

When inviting community members to engage in professional development, it is important to consider the following:

- Is the historical model a guide in the planning process?
- Do you have a space and time for each voice or representative of the community?
- Are multiple sources of media used to advertise events?
- Do you have a logo to brand the organization?
- Are events structured to allow members of the community to voice their opinions and share their knowledge?
- Have activities been included for student participation?
- Have awards been included?

### NOTES

1. www.rdi.emory.edu/index.html.
2. Evaluation report for Teaching in the Urban South, July 16, 2012, p. 1.

3. Evaluation report for Teaching in the Urban South, p. 2.
4. Evaluation report for Teaching in the Urban South, p. 3.
5. Evaluation report for Teaching in the Urban South, p. 3.

*Chapter Six*

# The Challenges of Implementing a Historical Model in a Contemporary Setting

Sheryl J. Croft and Tiffany D. Pogue

With little experience planning large-scale interventions like the TITUS in-itiative, the TITUS team and fellows were able to successfully replicate pieces of the historical model in a contemporary urban district. While the data compiled from conference attendee surveys suggest that the two-year TITUS initiative was a success, it was not without its challenges. Some challenges that emerged involved lack of finances, the need for creative recognition, and a realization that people need to be hungry for change. Collectively the team had to resolve issues related to the following:

- chronological re-creation of an organic process
- building trust
- ensuring authenticity in interactions
- the need for shared commitments
- lack of funding
- creative recognition of participants
- the need for people to be hungry for change
- the closing of a university department
- relocation of TITUS fellows

## CHRONOLOGICAL RE-CREATION OF AN ORGANIC PROCESS

From the outset, TITUS was never intended to be a research project with specific goals, hypotheses, and procedures. Rather, its purpose was to replicate a historical model used to educate children within an urban setting. As such, aspects of TITUS evolved as the university representative and TITUS team worked toward the collective purpose. Because TITUS was a pilot project, many of its activities occurred organically, and in this process, a chronological rendering fails to capture the synergy and spontaneity generated in the sessions. Perhaps the greatest challenge for this current book stems from the difficulty associated with recounting chronologically events that often occurred organically.

## Building Trust

One of the initial challenges that the TITUS team encountered resided in the ability of all members to trust student expertise and to engage them as equal partners. Admittedly, this egalitarian partnership was a departure from typical faculty–student interactions. Perhaps unique to the TITUS team, the graduate students brought to TITUS skills and talents derived from their prior experiences. Notwithstanding their unique talents, one of the barriers was to break down the typical student/teacher hierarchy and to rely on students as equals. Specifically, the egalitarian spirit grounded in trust for students' expertise, ideas, and experiences, while initially a challenge, eventually became the foundation on which the team's cooperation and collaboration were based.

## Ensuring Authenticity in Interactions

Another challenge resided in the insistence on authenticity of interactions. The question of authenticity became a concern when a team member scripted the responses of students during one of our first conferences. The scripting occurred out of a concern that students' voices would not be heard or received in an academic setting without prompting. In this case the desire for the audience to accurately *hear* student voices overrode the desire for authenticity. Dr. Peterson insisted that student voices be heard during the Noguera lecture:

> I asked them, "What is it that you really want to know? Are you interested in reframing it [your question]?" . . . It was important that their voices were heard. It was important that it came from them. This led to a discussion, which was like a session within a session.[1]

## Need for Shared Commitments

While the vast majority of those involved with the TITUS initiative shared a commitment to collaboration, not all did. In fact, after the final year, two fellows stopped participating in the initiative. We do not question these individuals' commitments to urban students, but suggest that they may not have bought into the historical model and the TITUS initiative. Further, one of the fellows who dropped out of the initiative was nominated by another fellow and as a result may not have been fully vested in the principles of TITUS.

## Lack of Funding

Despite the absence of a budget and university financial support, the TITUS initiative proved that finances did not hinder the work or define the success of collaboration. Instead, the team was amazed at how a small group of students, principals, and university personnel were able to accomplish so much with such meager resources.

Importantly, TITUS began with only the resources provided by the DES, in the form of paper and space. To mitigate the lack of funds, the team quickly discovered that by working through relationships, necessary resources were forthcoming. For example, one of the graduate students was able to secure folders and pens for the first conference. Another TITUS team member was able to persuade her spouse to draw the logo and tape many of the TITUS sessions. By contacting other members of the university at large, the TITUS team was able to publish posters, advertise the conference, and generate funds. Another donor offered the MARBL space, the special collections section of Woodruff Library, and refreshments for the reception held after the conference. In a similar fashion to the historical model, members outside of the team donated time and resources that compensated for the lack of financial resources.

## Creative Recognition of Participants

Additionally, the team learned the need to be creative with rewards. For example, the TITUS university representative taught about TITUS in a university course, and students (although they worked well beyond the hours of the course) obtained university credit. DES doctoral students gained experience for their CVs as TITUS professors teaching TITUS classes. Additionally, those who participated in the conference gained experience as faculty presenters. TITUS fellows nominated outstanding students to receive Horace Tate awards and certificates.

## Need for People to Be Hungry for Change

The TITUS initiative demonstrated that schools are hungry for the authentic assistance that universities can offer. When given an opportunity to work with individuals with shared commitment to and belief in the potential of urban students, stakeholders can come together to conquer seemingly insurmountable obstacles including poor funding, extreme time commitments, and logistical issues.

## Closing of the Division of Educational Studies and Student Relocation

The 2012 announcement of the eventual closing of Emory University's Division of Educational Studies had a significant impact on how the TITUS team functioned within DES. After the university announced the closing, some professors pondered their next steps as others assumed positions at other universities. With these moves, university interest and support for TITUS dwindled. Specifically, two professors left the department, two graduate students matriculated, and one moved to another state.

Amidst the change at the university, three TITUS fellows were reassigned to other schools. These reassignments were significant, because in one case a principal was reassigned from a middle school to a high school. This reassignment affected this principal's TITUS participation in that she had an entire new community to learn about. Another principal was reassigned to an elementary school; this assignment prohibited her TITUS involvement because TITUS delivered services to high schools and middle schools only. Finally, one principal resigned from the district. In the end, these challenges made it difficult for TITUS to function as originally designed. Nonetheless, TITUS continued.

## DIFFICULT TO WALK AWAY

The TITUS initiative formally ended shortly after the announced closing of the Division of Educational Studies. However, former team members still meet with fellows informally. In 2014, the American Educational Research Association featured a panel on TITUS, and a fellow flew to San Francisco to present with the team. TITUS was also featured on a panel during an international conference on urban education held in Jamaica. These professional appearances are also supplemented by the ongoing efforts of individual team members. One former undergraduate TITUS student commented, "After working with [students in a fellow's school] . . . I found that . . . TITUS sparked my passion . . . and with a bit of help I may be able to start a chapter of TITUS."

Today, the TITUS team members still meet as professional colleagues, most of whom populate universities at institutions throughout the South. Via email, virtual community apps, and personal exchanges, they continue to discuss the needs of urban schools and the ways their work within their new institutions can help meet those needs. In at least seven universities, former TITUS team members are discussing how to import TITUS into their university settings. The research agendas of at least some of the team members continue to be shaped by the TITUS experience.

Presently, some parents, TITUS team members, and other community members continue to inquire about the status of and the need for TITUS. A former TITUS student expressed the importance of continuing TITUS:

> I gained a passion for urban education and for finding ways to make it better for our students, no matter what state. . . . I learned that these are MY children and that I am accountable for them as much as they are accountable for themselves. It is my job to assist them in any way that I can so that they may be their best.[2]

Like the students, the TITUS team believes that with continued collaborative efforts from higher education and public school educators, a difference can be made in the lives and educational experiences of urban students. When asked about the overall value of TITUS, visiting professor Peterson summarized its impact with the following thoughts: "It served as a confirmation of the significance of educational advocacy and partnerships in education . . . between higher education and schools."[3]

## NOTES

1. Peterson, personal interview with author, November 7, 2015.
2. A. Smith, personal communication with author, May 6, 2015.
3. Peterson, personal interview with author, November 7, 2015.

# Final Words

In the final assessment of the TITUS initiative, one might ask whether TITUS really made a difference. During a presentation about TITUS at the 2013 AERA conference, fellow Greg Goodwin summarized his feelings about TITUS: "I am thankful for the grassroots effort of TITUS. My colleagues [fellows/principals] definitely benefited from the efforts of individuals [on the TITUS team] that actually wanted to make a difference in their community and took it upon themselves to make a difference."[1]

The university and school representatives, TITUS fellows, and other TITUS team members are themselves amazed at how a small group of committed students, principals, and university personnel could accomplish what they did by deliberately (and sometimes more organically) replicating an African American historical model of educational excellence in contemporary times. TITUS's success speaks to the power of a community committed—above all else—to the potential of urban students to learn and flourish through deliberate, shared efforts. Regarding TITUS's role in this, one parent concluded, "They may not be doing it perfectly. But as far as I can tell, this is the only space where we are all in here together."

The TITUS team's hope is that this book will serve as a guide for those seeking to recreate the model in their own communities.

## NOTE

1. G. Goodwin, presentation at the Annual Meeting of the American Educational Research Association, San Francisco, CA, April 27–May 1, 2013.

# Appendix A

**TITUS Fast Facts about Youth of Color in the United States and Georgia**[***]

| | ALL | White | Black | Latino | Asian | Native Amer. | Source and Year |
|---|---|---|---|---|---|---|---|
| Percentage of students suspended from public elementary or secondary schools during the 2005–2006 school year by race | 7 | 5 | 15 | 7 | 3 | 8 | *The Condition of Education 2009 Report*, Indicator 28, National Center for Educational Statistics |
| Percentage of 2010 high school seniors who have taken one AP exam during their high school career (can be used as a proxy for AP enrollment) | 28.3 | | 16.6 | 27 | | 14.2 | *7th Annual AP Report to the Nation*, College Board, 2011 |
| Percentage of 2010 high school seniors who have had a successful AP exam experience (score of 3 or higher) | 16.9 | | 3.9 | 14.6 | | 0.4 | *7th Annual AP Report to the Nation*, College Board, 2011 |
| ***Percentage of 2010 high school seniors who have had a successful AP exam experience (score of 3 or higher); for Georgia only | 19.1 | | 11.6 | 6.7 | | 0.04 | *7th Annual AP Report to the Nation*, College Board, 2011 |
| Average freshman graduation[a] rates by race for the 2005–2006 school year | | 80.6 | 57.6 | 68.7 | 89.9 | 61.8 | Common Core Data, ISE, National Center for Educational Statistics |

| | | | | | | | |
|---|---|---|---|---|---|---|---|
| ***Average freshman graduation rates by race for the 2005–2006 school year (Georgia only) | | 68 | 54.2 | 51.2 | 90 | 43.6 | Common Core Data, ISE, National Center for Educational Statistics |
| Percentage of students enrolled in elementary and secondary public schools labeled as gifted and talented in 2006 | 6.7 | 8 | 3.6 | 4.2 | 13.1 | 5.2 | National Center for Educational Statistics |
| ***Percentage of students enrolled in elementary and secondary public schools labeled as gifted and talented in 2006 (Georgia only) | 9.3 | 13.6 | 4.1 | 3.1 | 19.3 | 9.6 | National Center for Educational Statistics |
| Percentage of children ages 6–21 served under the Individuals with Disabilities Education Act in 2007 | 8.96 | 8.47 | 12.15 | 8.51 | 4.85 | 14.31 | *Status and Trends in the Education of Racial and Ethnic Minorities*, National Center for Educational Statistics, July 2010 |

| | | | | | | | |
|---|---|---|---|---|---|---|---|
| Percentage of children ages 6–21 served under the Individuals with Disabilities Education Act for Learning Disability in 2007 | 3.89 | 3.42 | 5.32 | 4.55 | 1.6 | 7.09 | *Status and Trends in the Education of Racial and Ethnic Minorities*, National Center for Educational Statistics, July 2010 |
| Percentage of children ages 6–21 served under the Individuals with Disabilities Education Act for Emotional Disturbance in 2007 | 0.67 | 0.62 | 1.27 | 0.41 | 0.18 | 1.11 | *Status and Trends in the Education of Racial and Ethnic Minorities*, National Center for Educational Statistics, July 2010 |
| Youth in residential custody (rates per 100,000) | 123 | 463 | 317 | | | | U.S. Department of Justice, Office of Juvenile Justice and Delinquency Prevention, Juvenile Justice Bulletin, December 2010 |

| | | | | | | | |
|---|---|---|---|---|---|---|---|
| Ethnic makeup of youth in residential custody | 35% | 32% | 24% | | | | U.S. Department of Justice, Office of Juvenile Justice and Delinquency Prevention, Juvenile Justice Bulletin, December 2010 |
| Average Critical Reading SAT score[b] (2008) | 502 | 528 | 430 | 454/ 456[c] | 513 | 485 | *Status and Trends in the Education of Racial and Ethnic Minorities*, National Center for Educational Statistics, July 2010 |
| Average Math SAT score (2008) | 515 | 537 | 426 | 463/ 453 | 581 | 491 | *Status and Trends in the Education of Racial and Ethnic Minorities*, National Center for Educational Statistics, July 2010 |

| Average Writing SAT score (2008) | 494 | 518 | 424 | 447/ 445 | 516 | 470 | *Status and Trends in the Education of Racial and Ethnic Minorities*, National Center for Educational Statistics, July 2010 |
|---|---|---|---|---|---|---|---|

\*\*\* Denotes information specific to Georgia.

a. Estimate of the percentage of an entering freshman class graduating in four years.

b. The SAT scores are for the entire test-taking population. They also have a dataset of "college-bound scores."

c. For Latino SAT scores, there are two numbers. The first number is the average for Mexican Americans; the second number is the average for Puerto Rican Americans. TITUS also had an average for all other Latinos, which always fell between Mexican and Puerto Rican Americans.

# Appendix B

## *Evaluation Report for TITUS Conference*

To: Professor Vanessa Siddle Walker
From: Fai Cheong
Title: An Evaluation Report for the Teaching in the Urban South (TITUS)
African American Excellence in Education Conference
Date: July 16, 2012

***

This report summarizes and analyzes participants' feedback regarding com-
munity–university partnership and their thoughts on their first African
American Excellence in Education Conference called by the Teaching in the
Urban South (TITUS) initiative. The event was held at Cedar Grove High
School on April 21, 2012.

Sixty-nine participants filled out a self-report questionnaire at the end of
the conference. Of the 69 respondents, 16 (23.5 percent) participated as
students, 12 (17.6 percent) as parents, 16 (23.5 percent) as teachers, 4 (5.9
percent) as school administrators, 2 (2.9 percent) as higher education faculty,
3 (4.4 percent) as higher education administrators, and 2 (2.9 percent) both as
teachers and parents or teachers and community members. Thirteen (19.1
percent) participated in other roles such as guests, community leaders, volunteers, etc. *The results suggested that the group consisted of diverse participants and stakeholders.*

The respondents answered three 5-point rating scales to express their
views on the relative importance of the conceptual grounding and supporting

activities of the TITUS initiative (1 = not important at all, and 5 = most important). Most respondents considered it very important to connect school communities and higher education institutions in order to improve education ($M = 4.6$, $SD = .522$). They also viewed the levels of participation by both students and parents as of great importance in the community–university partnership ($M = 4.8$, $SD = .445$). *The results indicated that in general, respondents valued community–university partnership and the use of awards in educational improvement.*

The respondents also rated their levels of agreement to statements on how well the various aspects of the conference were run using an Agree/Disagree 5-point Likert response scale (1 = Strongly Disagree to 5 = Strongly Agree). There was on average a strong agreement on a) the effectiveness of the opening session of the conference in providing a clear overview and under-standing of its purpose ($M = 4.68$, $SD = .621$); b) the important role of the town hall meeting in fostering the community and higher education partner-ship ($M = 4.64$, $SD = .598$); c) the availability of suitable session choices ($M = 4.67$, $SD = .641$); d) the high quality of organizational aspects of the conference ($M = 4.79$, $SD = 4.46$); and e) the high quality of the setting and catering of the conference ($M = 4.78$, $SD = 4.56$). *The findings provided very positive ratings of the various aspects of the conference.*

The respondents chose to attend one to two sessions on various topics in history, science, literacy, gender-based education, college preparation, and more. On average, they agreed across all the sessions that the units were informative and useful ($M = 4.82$, $SD = .443$). As indicated, all the values of the mean ratings were close to 5. *The positive average ratings suggested high levels of instructional efficacy in individual sessions.*

The respondents shared their thoughts and comments on the conference and the TITUS initiative in their replies to five open-ended questions.

The first question solicited comments on aspects of the conference that the respondents liked most and found most useful. Specific notice and acco-lades were given to Professor Siddle Walker's presentation on the history of education. Respondents identified the presence of, engagement of, and inter-actions and collaborations among different stakeholders (students, parents, teachers) as useful aspects. Some identified the individual sessions that they had attended, such as the ones on gender-based and science education, as very useful.

The second question collected information on aspects of the conference that respondents liked the least and found the least useful. Many responses indicated that there were none that they liked the least; all of them were useful. Two respondents listed the concurrent sessions during lunch as their "least liked and useful" answers; one wrote down the town hall and one the presentation portion as their replies. Two identified the time allotted to the opening and the award ceremony and thought they were "long." Finally, one commented on the choice of titles and topics and suggested that "less college style titles/topics, [and] more student/parent/teacher topics" would have been useful. This response may suggest a preference for more emphasis on practical applications.

The third question asked for input for new sessions to include in future conferences. The responses were related to session topics, formats, and participants.

a. The following are the suggestions regarding topics: disciplinary sessions, motivation, engagement, data-guided decision-making, parents' involvement, leadership, gender-based classrooms, engineering education for African Americans, importance of economics and foreign languages, heroes, family, instructional strategies for different types of students, funding, diversity, girls and their roles, education of other minorities such as Latinos and Asians, advocacy, bullying, career education, parenting skills, literacy, curriculum and politics, parental support of teachers, peer pressure, and college preparation.
b. Recommendations regarding formats are as follows: field trips, hands-on and culturally relevant activities, round table discussions by students, and more collaboration between students and instructors.
c. Proposed ideas regarding participants include having sessions with district-level administrators and politicians as well as more parental involvement.

The fourth question was concerned with proposed measures to improve the quality and effectiveness of the conference and programs. There were responses stating, "Everything was great!" and "None." Four major themes or groups of ideas were identified in the recommendations. The first one was a call for more publicity and to "increase notification through community newspapers and newsletters to increase stakeholder involvement." A related theme was to involve "gov't people" and more parents. The third was to have a greater focus on identifying solutions to existing problems. The last suggestion was for more time in each session.

The final question asked the respondents to share other additional thoughts or comments that they felt were important. There were a lot of complimentary responses on the conferences and the organizers and presenters, much encouragement and anticipation of continued commitment and activities, and expression of interest in participation. For example, a parent wrote "I think overall this was an eye opener for me and I will definitely pass this information along to my fellow parents." One respondent suggested that more parental involvement was needed. Another respondent suggested that he/she was "faced with a slightly elitist attitude by one" graduate student and he/she wished that "the Emory students were more open/friendly."

*Summary and conclusions: Based on the data collected on the African American Excellence in Education: Reclaiming the Past, Preparing for the Future Conference, TITUS was very successful in recruiting the intended target population, providing a space for many groups of stakeholders to interact with each other, introducing and gathering support for its initiative, organizing and running smoothly an event in a public school, delivering informative and useful sessions on various topics in urban education, and soliciting useful feedback and input from participants. Participant responses across all demographics suggest an impressively high perception of the overall quality, efficacy, importance, and usefulness of the TITUS initiative and an increased interest in future participation and additional topics of discussion. It can reasonably be estimated that the positive impact of the sessions, organization, and overall goal of the conference extended beyond the participants. Word of mouth, coupled with helpful suggestions, demonstrated a continued interest in such conferences, and the recommendations regarding a need for increased awareness, publicity, and media exposure suggest that participants' positive experiences are transferable to new participants and additional demographics. The suggestions for improvement were minimal and the positive feedback was so heavily weighted toward the highest end of scale, implying that organizers, contributors, and supporters were successful in achieving their goals and objectives.*

# Glossary

**African American Pedagogical Model (AAPM):** a model based on V. Walker's research on pre-*Brown* principals.

**deliverables:** the services requested by the fellows (principals) and the services the university was able to provide based on available resources.

**Division of Educational Studies (DES):** During the course of the TITUS initiative, the Division of Educational Studies, a part of Emory University's College of Arts and Sciences, served both undergraduate and graduate students in its master's and PhD programs. Offering programs that emphasized a disciplinary approach to education in urban and comparative issues, the Division "provided students with a foundation for understanding the social and cultural context in which education occurs and for interpreting relationships among education, the individual, and society" retrieved http://des.emory.edu/home/about/index.html. *Emory University has announced the closing of DES, effective August 31, 2017.*

**school liaisons:** school insiders, persons designated by the TITUS fellows to work directly with TITUS team members to organize university deliverables.

**school representative:** the person who, because of her insider status within the school system, served to vet TITUS fellows and work with the university representative as a liaison between the TITUS team and TITUS fellows.

**TITUS fellows:** the initial seven principals of urban Title I schools who were recruited and vetted based on the AAPM principles and values.

**TITUS liaisons:** the TITUS team members assigned to specific TITUS fellows to provide deliverables.

**TITUS team:** composed of graduate students, other professors, and the university representative.

**university representative:** originally the founder and person on whose research the TITUS initiative was based; now includes a senior scholar from the university who serves as a contact person and representative for the university.

# Index

AAPM. *See* African American Pedagogical Model

ACSS. *See* Association of Colleges and Secondary Schools

AERA. *See* American Educational Research Association

African American Pedagogical Model (AAPM), 1, 4, 9, 16, 20, 32; keynote address about, 44; professional development workshops discussion and chart use of, 12–14, 13

African American professional network: idea dissemination in, xxii; influence of, xxiii; meeting structure of, xxii; overview of, xxi; professional development activities of, xxi–xxii; student and teacher achievement recognition in, xxvii; student meeting inclusion of, xxvii; as TITUS foundation, xxvii

American Educational Research Association (AERA), 20, 56, 59

American Teachers Association (ATA), xx, xxiii, xxiv

Association of Colleges and Secondary Schools (ACSS), xx; black children needs commitment of, xxv–xxvi; Black student issues in, xxiii–xxiv; conversational topics of, xxiii; high school principals and university professionals meeting attendance at, xxiv; student-teacher identification in, xxiii; teacher community involvement in, xxiii

ATA. *See* American Teachers Association

Bass, Lisa, 30–31

Benford, Pam, 31, 39, 42, 48

Black educators: African American professional network overview of, xxi; black children needs commitment of, xxv–xxvi; commitments of, xxii–xxiii; as examples for students, xxv; higher education and public school leader collaboration of, xxiv–xxv; high performance insistence of, xx; job loss fear of, xix–xx; meeting structure of, xxii; organizational network of, xx; problem-solving responsibility of, xxvi–xxvii; professional development activities of, xxi–xxii; in segregation era, xix; shared commitment and promise of, xxv; state-based pedagogical networks creation of, xx. *See also* teachers

Black schools, xxiii, xxv, xxvi; history of inequality in, xix; parental support for, 15

Bond, Horace Mann, xix, xxii, xxiv

*Brown v. Board of Education*, xx, xxiii, 7n2

Byas, Ulysses, xx; on Black children commitment, 14; on Black educators responsibility, xxvi–xxvii; curricular survey of, xxvi

Cozart, Leland, xix, xxiii
Croft, Sheryl J., 45

Davis, Allison, xxii, xxiii, xxiv
deliverables, 19, 27, 28, 29, 32, 33
Division of Educational Studies (DES), xxiii, 2, 4, 36, 55, 56; closure of, 49; mission statement of, 19–20; TITUS team impact of closure in, 56; Twenty-First Century Position Paper of, 1; urban education commitment of, 1–2
Dove, Pearlie, 50

Emory University, 36, 56; DES at, xxiii, 1, 2; school systems surrounding, 7n1; TITUS fellow distinction of, 4, 11; TITUS program of, xxiii, xxvii

Facebook, 36
"From the Kitchen to the Classroom" conference, 48; events threatening of, 49; highlights of, 49; researcher and practitioner subject-area panels in, 50; school liaison disinterest in, 49; student participation in, 49; town hall session in, 50

Georgia Teachers and Education Association (GTEA): meetings of, xxi–xxii; meeting structure of, xxii; professional development activities of, xxi–xxii
Goodwin, Greg, 31, 33, 39–40, 48, 59
Governor's Office of Student Achievement, Georgia, 7n1
GTEA. *See* Georgia Teachers and Education Association

*Hello Professor* (Walker), xx, xxvi
*Herald*, xxi, xxvi
Hinnant-Crawford, Brandi, 45

Johnson, Latrice P., 45
Johnson, Mordecai W., xxiii, xxiv, xxv

Jones, Amber, 45
Juergensen, Miyoshi, 30, 45

King, Martin Luther, Jr., xxii

Lovejoy, Owen R., xxiii, xxv

National Colored PTA, 15
National Pan-Hellenic Council, 39
Noguera, Pedro, 29, 35, 37, 39, 41; lecture of, 39–40, 54; reflections on lecture of, 40
Noguera Conference, 37

parents: black schools support of, 15; "Reclaiming the Model of African American Excellence in Education" conference session for, 48; segregated education support of, 15; TITUS professional development workshops involvement of, 15, 16
Pogue, Tiffany D., 45
Powell, Adam Clayton, xxii
principals: ACSS meeting attendance of, xxiv; as TITUS fellow, 4, 6; in university-public school collaboration, 4, 5, 6
professional development and community engagement, xxi–xxii, xxiii, 31, 67–68; collaborative opportunities in, 37; Facebook use for, 36; flyer use for, 36–37, 38, 41; "From the Kitchen to the Classroom" conference for, 48–50; ideas to consider in, 50; media creation and use for, 36; multidirectional flow of knowledge in, 37; Noguera lecture as, 39; Noguera lecture success in, 40; press releases for, 37; "Reclaiming the Model of African American Excellence in Education" school-based conference theme for, 42–43, 44–48; school-based conference delivery shape, 43–44; social media use in, 35, 36; stakeholder participation in, 37–39; student voices in, 40; TITUS community outreach activity participation for, 37; TITUS fellow talks in, 39–40; two events for, 37–39

professional development workshops, TITUS, 9; additional parental involvement creation in, 16; African American Pedagogical Model discussion and chart use in, 12–14, 13; Black children needs commitment in, 13–14; Black parental support in segregated era discussion in, 15; Byas poem used in, 14; contemporary dialogue on "lost" model in, 12; current activities in historical context of, 15; Emory University special relationship in, 11; exchange of ideas climate creation in, 9; fellows "safe space" meeting preference for, 10; fellows' secretaries communication in, 10–14; ideas to consider in, 16–17; materials inclusion in, 11; meeting space search in, 9–10; preparation details in, 12; professional relationship building in, 16; room preparation for, 11; self-selection lunch preferences for, 10–11; table arrangement for, 11–12; traditional norms of respect following in, 10; travel plan discussion for, 11; "trickster" motif discussion in, 14

Race and Difference Initiative (RDI), 39
"Reclaiming the Model of African American Excellence in Education" conference, 44; evaluations of, 48; meals and student awards in, 48; multilayered responsibilities in, 45; opening session of, 47; others' voices respect message of, 46–47; participants at, 45; professional development sessions in, 47; school-based conference theme of, 42–43, 43; structure of, 45; team and fellow collaboration on, 44; TITUS award application example for, 42; town hall and parent session in, 48. *See also* TITUS conference evaluation report
relationship building, 16, 30
Robinson, W. A., xxiii

School Master's Club of Georgia, problem-solving survey collaboration efforts of, xxvi

school representative, 2–4, 6, 7n3, 28–29, 59
segregated education: Black educators in, xix; Black parental support in, 15; high performance in, xx; lack of resources in, xxvi
Southern Association of Colleges and Secondary Schools, xx, xxvi
students, 2; ACSS issues of, xxiii–xxiv; African American professional network achievement recognition of, xxvii; African American professional network meeting inclusion of, xxvii; black educators as examples for, xxv; "From the Kitchen to the Classroom" conference participation of, 49; "Reclaiming the Model of African American Excellence in Education" conference awards of, 48; teacher identification with, xxiii; TITUS team regarding, 19, 20, 21, 54, 56; voices in professional development and community engagement of, 40

teachers: African American professional network achievement recognition of, xxvii; community involvement of, xxiii; student identification with, xxiii
Teaching in the Urban South (TITUS), xxiii, 1, 2; African American professional network foundation of, xxvii; authentic university assistance in, 55–56; camaraderie in meetings of, 23–24; educational partners in, 22; final assessment of, 59; formal end of, 56–57; former team members continuation of, 56–57; historical model needs of, 19; intentionality of, 22; intragroup accountability in, 24; logo creation for, 23; purpose of, 53–54; university representative vision for, 2. *See also* professional development workshops; university-public school collaboration
team-fellow liaison, 28, 49; assignment of, 28; "fellow packets" creation in, 29; first meeting talking points for, 29–30; Goodwin and Benford on role of, 31; ideas to consider for, 33–34; ongoing

communication and email example of, 30–31; relationship building in, 30; school community resource identification by, 31; school representative first school meeting for, 28–29; service delivery and communication of, 33; superintendent letter and conversation script for, 29

TITUS. *See* Teaching in the Urban South

TITUS conference evaluation report: additional thoughts on, 69–70; community-university partnership valued in, 67–68; diverse participants and stakeholders in, 67; format recommendations on, 69; ideas for participants in, 69; improvement measures for, 69; instructional efficacy in sessions on, 68; new session topics suggestions on, 69; participant feedback in, 67; positive ratings on aspects of, 68; respondents on least useful aspects of, 68–69; respondents on useful aspects of, 68; summary and conclusions on, 70

TITUS fellow, 29; Emory University distinction of, 4, 11; principals as, 4, 6; professional development and community engagement talks of, 39–40; "Reclaiming the Model of African American Excellence in Education" conference collaboration of, 44; "safe space" meeting preference of, 10; secretaries communication regarding, 10–14; TITUS team regarding, 27, 31, 56. *See also* team-fellow liaison

TITUS team, 44, 59; conception and implementation ownership of, 22; DES closing and student relocation impact on, 56; DES mission statement use in, 19–20; doctoral students prior experience for, 20; doctoral students relationship as, 19; educational partners in, 22; fellow service needs reviewed by, 31; fellows reassignment impacting, 56; fellows specific needs addressed by, 27; financial resource lack challenge of, 55; food sharing of, 24; former members continuation as, 56–57; ideas

to consider in, 25; intentionality of, 22; intragroup accountability of, 24; issue resolving of, 53; liaison model creation of, 28; logo creation of, 23; meeting camaraderie of, 23–24; other service provider identification of, 32; participant recognition of, 55; professional appearances of, 56; as "professional with previous experiences", 22–23; public school skepticism review of, 2; SAT workshop of, 33; service delivery plan of, 32; services and member qualifications of, 32; shared commitments challenge of, 54–55; small-group discussions in, 20; student as equals on, 54; student identification of, 21; student voices challenge of, 54; trust building challenge of, 54; urban school experiences of, 21–22; urban student help desire of, 21; values and commitments of, 20; visiting scholars in, 20–21. *See also* professional development and community engagement; team-fellow liaison

"trickster" motif, 14

trust building, 5, 54

Tumblr, 36

Twenty-First Century Position Paper, 1

Twitter, 36

university-public school collaboration, xxiv–xxv; common beliefs of representatives in, 3; DES Twenty-First Century Position Paper on, 1; doctoral students voice in, 2; ideas to consider in, 7; K-12 bridge building of, 2; list of school needs in, 6; principals as TITUS fellows in, 4, 6; principal selection criteria for, 4; school representative job in, 3–4; structure requirements of, 1; TITUS team review of public school skepticism in, 2; university and public school representative linking in, 2–3, 7n3; university and school representative letter crafting in, 4; university and school representative school visits in, 6; university help to principals in, 6; university representative respect for principals in, 5; university representative school visits in, 6; university representative TITUS vision for, 2; university representative trust and credibility building in, 5; urban education commitment of, 1–2

university representative, 2–3, 4, 5–6, 7n3, 59

Walker, Vanessa Siddle, xx, xxvi, 46, 68
WordPress, 36

# About the Editors

**Sheryl J. Croft** is an assistant professor in the department of educational leadership at Kennesaw State University, where she is also coordinator of the Educational Doctorate (EdD) program. She has also been the director of Teaching in the Urban South (TITUS) since its inception in 2011. Her work focuses on the impact of policy on public education, historical models of leadership, and collaborations between higher education and P–12 school leaders. Her research foci are educational reform, university/college collaborations, and contemporary leadership in marginalized populations. She has presented in international, national, and local venues. With over thirty-five years' experience working in P–12 urban districts, serving in roles from teacher to principal to assistant superintendent, her work focuses on facilitating connections between K–12 and university partners as well as working to improve educational opportunities for all students, particularly marginalized populations.

**Tiffany D. Pogue** is an assistant professor of teacher education at Albany State University. Her research interests include participatory literacy communities, culturally relevant teaching, hip hop–based education, and community engagement. As program coordinator for Education Foundations and Graduate Programs, Pogue has helped design pre-service classes and programs intended to increase students' efficacy, literacy skills, and levels of community engagement. Her interdisciplinary research has been published in journals and encyclopedias. She has also presented at local, national, and international professional conferences. Dr. Pogue is the founder of HBCU Prof, an institution dedicated to celebrating and providing resources for faculty at Historically Black Colleges and Universities. She currently serves as co-director of Teaching in the Urban South (TITUS), and is the director of the Academy for Future Teachers at Albany State University. She received the Best New Researcher Award from *Written Communication* in 2015.

**Vanessa Siddle Walker** is the Samuel Candler Dobbs Professor of Educational Studies at Emory University. For twenty-nine years, she has explored the segregated schooling of African American children, considering sequentially the climate that permeated southern schools (*Their Highest Potential*), the network of professional collaborations that explained the similarity of these schools (*Hello Professor*), and the hidden systems of advocacy that sought equality and justice (*Hidden Provocateurs*, New Press, Spring 2018). Her historical research has appeared in journals such as the *Harvard Educational Review, Review of Education Research, American Educational Research Journal, Educational Research*, and *Teachers College Record*, and her assessment of the implications of this history for contemporary settings appears in *Facing Racism in Education, Racing Moral Formation*, and*Living the Legacy*. Walker is a recipient of the prestigious Grawemeyer Award in Education, the AERA Early Career Award, three AERA SIG awards, and two awards from other professional associations. She lectures in a variety of community, national, collegiate, and international settings, including delivering the annual AERA *Brown v. Board of Education* Lecture in 2012. Walker received her training in education at the University of North Carolina at Chapel Hill and the Harvard Graduate School of Education.

# About the Contributors

**Brandi Hinnant-Crawford**, PhD, is an assistant professor of educational research at Western Carolina University. Brandi has degrees from North Carolina State University, Brown University, and Emory University. An aspiring scholar-activist, Brandi conducts research that seeks to uncover best practices in policy-making and instructional pedagogies for marginalized communities.

**Latrise P. Johnson** was born, raised, and educated in Atlanta, Georgia. She attended Morris Brown College and Georgia State University, and completed her PhD at Emory University in 2012. Dr. Johnson is an assistant professor at the University of Alabama, where she teaches undergraduate and graduate courses in secondary English language arts and literacy. She is also professor in residence at a local high school, where she teaches creative writing to 10th and 11th graders. Her work focuses on writing and the literacy experiences of students at the margins. She has published work in *Urban Education*, *Research in the Teaching of English*, and numerous other journals. Dr. Johnson lives with her wife and daughter in Tuscaloosa, Alabama.

**Amber Jones** is currently the Founding African American Literature Teacher at KIPP St. Louis High School in Missouri. Dr. Jones graduated from Emory in 2016 after earning her PhD in educational studies. In her new position, Dr. Jones relies upon the vision and training she received as a member of the research team and Division of Educational Studies (DES) family to teach a culturally relevant high school literacy curriculum to underserved populations.

**Miyoshi Juergensen** is an educator whose work focuses on educational processes that bridge opportunity gaps for marginalized student populations. She is a graduate of North Carolina Central University and earned her doctorate in educational studies from Emory University. As a former classroom teacher and scholar concerned with students of color on the margins of success, she examines how educators—African American educators in particular—have responded to dropouts from historical and contemporary perspectives. Given her experience with instructional technologies that positively impact students' academic outcomes, Miyoshi is currently the instructional technology coach for secondary schools for the Tuscaloosa City Schools system, where she works closely with public school educators and students to enhance teaching and learning. Miyoshi is also an adjunct professor of educational foundations and multicultural education courses in the department of social and cultural studies at the University of Alabama. She lives with her wife and daughter in Tuscaloosa, Alabama.